T0116395

ANTHOLOGY of AWFUL VERSE

MAXWELL GORDON

 www.trafford.com

North America & international
toll-free: 1 888 232 4444 (USA & Canada)
fax: 812 355 4082

ANTHOLOGY OF AWFUL VERSE
MAXWELL GORDON

FOREWORD AT THE BACK
[WHY RHYME? WHY VERSIFY AT ALL?]

PART 1

STRANGE PEOPLE & STRANGE EVENTS

ON THE ANTIQUITY OF FLEAS

THE EPIC POEM BELOW
IS REPUTED TO BE THE
SHORTEST IN EXISTENCE.
IT DOES NOT CLAIM TO
BE AN ORIGINAL WORK
OF THE AUTHOR, BEING
DEEPLY ROOTED IN THE
SOIL OF EARLIEST TIME.

Adam
Had'em!

P.S.   READ ON AT YOUR RISK.
WHAT FOLLOWS IS WORSE!

THE SNAIL'S GRIM PROGRESS
AS OBSERVED BY A CASUAL CAMPER

Before I could slide into sleep
    One latish warm evening of summer
Strange creatures decided to creep
    Up the side of my tent, - two in number,

Not making much progress, but still
    Intent upon having a race
Each one being slowed down by its shell
    Revealing not much of its face

Apart from twin horns that those creatures
    From out of their foreheads protrude.
But what are those odd-looking features
    Are they feeling around for their food?

If feelings they have, they conceal them,
    No! They're actually eyes on long stalks!
As for legs, they will never reveal them
    For a snail only crawls, never walks.

Behind each, those silvery trails
    Leave unmistakable traces
One expects of such slithery snails
    At snail's-pace competing in races.

On racing they seemed so intent
    So why should I wish them disturbed?
They would hardly endanger my tent,
    So why not sleep-on unperturbed?

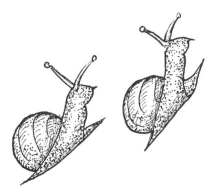

But just before turning away
    To dream of some lesser event,
The snail in the lead fell away,
    No longer to mess-up my tent!

Some gust of the wind had him shaken,
    From the sides of the tent as they flapped
His every ambition forsaken,
    At climbing he felt no more apt.

Thought I, if some high-flown ambition
    To take one's first place in a race
Then fall from a top-most position
    One would dive to the depths of disgrace.

But out from my sleeping-bag squirming,
    At last coming out of my shell,
I cautiously stood up, avoiding
    The chance I might stand on that snail.

Then carefully lifted the fallen one
    To take him outside and to grass;
His fate would be such an appalling one
    If one should unwittingly pass

While walking on wet grass with shoes on,
　　Then sounds the occasional crunch,
Be you sure that some snail you have stood on.
　　Are you tempted to have him for lunch?

Next morning, the grass was all dewy,
　　I saw that the snail had progressed
Unharmed and unhurried, - still chewey
　　If a snail one should wish to digest.

That pet-snail I thenceforth called Margot,
　　Pronounced with an unpronounced "T";
The French call their snails "les ESCARGOTS"
　　And serve them fried-up for their tea.

They plop them in water to boil them,
　　Then out of their shells do they wrench them
Next, fry them in oil to embroil them
　　In what is by method a French one.

From the story, two morals arise:
(1)　　Our human race moves far too fast!
The snail that was slower was wise
　　Being unhurried. The winner came last!

(2)　Think not all success is sublime;
　　Could be our own fault if we flop
And end up a mess in the slime
　　For we've farther to fall from the top!

What is worse, should you feel so depressed
　　That life fails to bring you much good on,
There's always some ill-wishing pest,
　　Who'd add to your woes saying, "GET STOOD ON!"

JUST ONCE IN A BLUE-MOON
AN ACTUAL SIGHTING IN LATE AUGUST 1950

"Good heavens! The sun's turned blue, turned blue!"
    That's what I didn't say, because
The mates who worked with me, - I knew
    Would say "He's crackers, - always was!"

Well hid amongst the trees, commissioned
    To gather, for the Forestry,
From low-down branches, seeds sufficient
    To fill big canvas bags, - us three.

Just trees, trees, trees, - of sky a glimpse,
    Was all we saw from where we gathered,
Till stepping on the pathway once,
    I saw the scene still far from fathomed.

"Come out a moment on the pathway,
    Just tell me what *you* see, you two."
They slowly trudged out, standing half-way,
    "Good heavens, it seems the sun's turned blue!"

As on we worked till time to stop
    Perplexed by what we'd seen,
The sun shone on past ten o'clock
    Bright BLUE, as sure as trees are green!

Arriving home round five or six,
    A soldier tall, American,
Approached me, - said he'd come to fix
    Some problem with his jerrycan.

6

"Say, sonny, does your Scarrish sun
    Shine always blooo?" his question asking.
I answered him, of course for fun,
    "No, - normally Royal Stewart tartan!"

That evening, happening quite naturally,
    To give the moon its rightful place,
The sun dipped down just gradually,
    But left behind its true-blue face.

The moon was just as blue, or more-so,
    But no mere apparition was it, if
In far-south England, Paris, - all saw,
    That same phenomenon, - as positive.

Most miracles have explanations
    For driving men-of-science frantic:
High clouds, of forest-fires creations,
    Being blown from far across th'Atlantic,

Made sure both sun and moon were seen
    By folks from far and wide and human,
With clouds of dense-blue smoke between,
    As happens once in every BLUE-MOON!

DORMITORY DISCORD
EVENT OCCURRING AT A YOUTH HOSTEL

A Hostel meant for youthful folks
Should be for all back-packing blokes,
Whatever age, type, or persuasion,
A friendly place of toleration -

Until the dormitory reveals
Exactly how each dorm-mate feels
When roused from slumber by phenomena
The likes of which could not be commoner.

"SHUT UP, my man, you've just been snoring!"
So said the chap I'd been ignoring
By having slept, and slept profoundly
Midst many dormitory mates around me.

He even rose from bed to poke me,
And this was what of course awoke me.
Aware of others doing the same,
Said I, "No, no," and slept again.

Once more resounded sonorous snorings.
From bunks in double range of storeys
Again I felt that poke of wrath;
Again I said, "No, no. Ger'off!

Just listen to that prattling noise
Of *others* rattling adenoids
Which had annoyed you. Hear those sonic
Sounds presented polyphonic!"

So rising from his bed, he digs
Those snorting pigs between their ribs,
By which indignant digs of violence
He bids them be condemned to silence.

Those sleepers did he so abhor
So horribly disposed to snore
Quite unawares, while making this
Complaint that caused his wakefulness.

SNORTED RETORT

"Aha, my friend, you really ought to
Consult a fellow-feeling doctor
Who'd cure you of your need to stay
Awake, - such snorings to survey.

He may an antidote prescribe,
Pink pills, or potion to imbibe,
A pair of ear-plugs might be fine
To shut out snores from snoozing swine."

CONCLUSIVE OBSERVATION

The next day, he'd gone off before us;
Next night! - Oh, what a snorers' chorus!
Had he just stayed as numbers doubled,
He'd be dismayed and doubly troubled!

Intentionally I stayed awake
To witness how much noise they'd make.
At least six snorting dormant devils
Were snoring at abnormal levels,

Which led me to the sure conclusion
Non-snoring is but false illusion,
Each person with a mouth endowed
Is prone to snore, and snore aloud.

The surest cure for mouths wide open
Is slyly shove a bar of soap in.
This won't prevent the snorer's wrath,
But will foment much foaming froth!

FATAL FATE OF FLY

A 'fly cup of tea' is taken to be
A cup that's taken on the sly,
At least in the land I once was born in,
And not a cup that a fly has fallen in.

A chap who'd come across from France
Was hardly pleased when, quite by chance,
A passing fly, to him "une mouche",
Was nearly swallowed "dans sa bouche".

For it had fallen in his cup
Just as he raised it to his lip,
Much worse if, downed amongst the dregs,
Had it been drowned on its last legs.

Each leg so limp, so loosely folded,
Not merely drenched, but badly scalded,
My friend perhaps complained because
He knew not just how pained it was.

He dragged that fly from out his cup,
No dragon-fly one might wash-up,
But just an ordinary creature,
Whose face had turned so sad a feature!

Take comfort, friend, it was not thee
That perished in that cup of tea,
But one small creature knocked quite senseless
With all six legs left quite defenceless.

So next time that you see a fly
Fly by your cup, advise it why
In water much too hot for him
It should avoid its daily swim.

UNINTENDED EXIT FROM BUS

One garrulous Glaswegian, great of girth,
    Got hoisted up aboard a bus,
Or should we say a coach, to state its worth,
    Long-distance journey, labelled thus:

"To London" - full four-hundred miles of journey.
    The passengers had settled down,
For, scheduled to arrive next day quite early,
    They sought some chance for sleeping sound.

Our fat Glaswegian friend might sleep eventually,
    Though not from natural exhaustion,
But brought about by booze perpetually;
    His cause turned out to be a lost yin.

The driver revved the coach's engine, - barrrm!
    But first he warned the drunken oaf
To sit down peacefully or else he'd bar him
    From further travel, - chuck him off.

He'd paid his fare, paid not the slightest heed
    But staggered up and down the passage
Conversing with whoever bent his heid
    To listen to his blustered message.

Some tried being nice, while others turned away,
    Or simulated sleep while craving
Some peace and quiet, sincerely as they'd pray
    The lout would cease his loud-mouthed raving.

"How are ye, Hen? Enjoying the journey? My!
    A long way lies in front o'ye!"
Noo, mind that fellah sat beside ye, - why?
    Just dinnae let yer man get on tae ye!"

With every utterance growing the more unseemly,
    Descending into language foul,
Still louder did he speak his spiel obscenely,
    Until the driver heard him growl:

"Excuthe me, Mithter," so the drunkard spoke,
    "I need the lavvy, my guid fellah,
Wull ye jist let me aff, at the next stoap?"
    The passengers gave praise to Allah!

The driver duly did as he was bidden;
    The sozzled one still rambled on.
"You'll find the toilet round that corner hidden."
    The next stop being at Hamilton.

The engine shuddered to a standstill sudden
    As came his moment of relief.
He staggered out of sight on business urgent,
    But on emerging, great his grief!

While off attending to that pressing need
    And after scarcely six short seconds,
Quite unaware the driver paid no heed,
    For "Fare is fair" he rightly reckoned.

His starter pressed, he pressed on through the night,
    Ex-passenger left standing stranded,
While all slept soundly on till day-break's light.
    Their captain would they have commended,

But commendations none had he to face,
    As well observed had been the custom:
Another driver'd come to take his place, -
    Just half-way had the first one bussed'em!

TRAIN-SPOTTING: IT TAKES ALL TYPES TO TRAVEL ON A TRAIN!
OBSERVING ONE'S ODD FELLOW-PASSENGERS, - BUT SELDOM
STOPPING TO CONTEMPLATE ONE'S OWN PERSONAL ODDNESS.

REGARDING THE ROCKING ROCK-FAN

Just next to me while travelling on the train
Sat one with something rattling in his brain;
A metal cow-clap lay upon his lap,
Thin wires connecting-up to that strange chap.

Those wires required each one a plastic plug,
Each plug required for shoving in each lug,
By which device continuously he'd rock
Both back and forth, and forth and back, non-stop.

His bobbing bonce kept nodding noddingly
In constant time with all that canned monotony;
Whatever melody it bore, if worth repeating,
Lay stored below that boring blatant beating . . .

All mass-produced, as music masquerading
For empty cavities of brains invading.
One wished the wierdo-world of that same chappie
Fulfilled his needs, and kept him tame and happy.

PURELY PERSONAL PREFERENCES

A Symphony of Brahms perhaps, for vast
Variety of musical contrast
Need I to elevate my spirit higher?
And fan my feeble intellectual fire.

KNITTER KNITTING NEEDFULLY

Over there, that pretty little lady sitting
Was busy doing her knitting, knitting, knitting,
As if unwittingly she knitted heedlessly
By no means were her needles knitting needlessly,

For as her fingers itched so skilfully
To have emplaced each stitch so fittingly,
Her needles needing them for pulling wool over,
Indeed the net result would be a pullover.

GOGGLING AT GORGEOUS GIRLS

A girl, once gorgeous, sat across the corridor
Cosmetics in excess had made her fair face horrider
She'd dyed her hair which made it look so sickly,
And made her lips unkissable with lipstick thickly.

Another girl, more gorgeous, knew she needed
No false cosmetics, as she had succeeded
To keep her beauty blessed by mother nature,
Thus pristine freshness blessed her every feature.

TELEPHONING CEASELESSLY

A grinning girl across from me, alone,
Like many more, had grabbed a hand-held phone
Through which she seldom ceased to conversate
But seemed to miss the means to contemplate.

Ah! what is life if full of force-fed care
We have no time to sit or stand and stare
And just say, "Arr, arr, arr, arr, arr, arr."
Imagining how civilised we are, are, are!

PRE-PLATFORM PANDEMONIUM

Next stop approached, the train-speed slowly lowered;
Already several passengers aboard
Were stretching hands towards those high-up racks
Above their heads so they could grab their bags.

"Watch out dear lady! - leave this one to me
I'll get it for you." - "Thank you sir, said she."
For otherwise it would, like her old self,
Have probably been left upon the shelf.

A man less slim from out his seat appears;
It seemed he hadn't seen his feet for years.
"Get out the way! Just see how fat am I."
A lamp-bulb-shape graced his anatomy.

The exit door being just about to slide,
He pushed all other passengers aside,
Soon seen to struggle as he dragged his fat form
Plus all his luggage, lugged along the platform.

NEXT STOP

More passengers poured in, all types and sizes,
To stare at other folk it seldom wise is, -
Yet can a person help being fascinated
By such strange fashions as had some created?

One finds a little time to just compare styles
Of different people's very varied hair-styles.
Good heavens! There goes one with spikey tufts
All hell let loose with gel and such-like stuffs!

Another, bowing to a different god,
Had sacrificed his curls to look as odd
As possible, exposing close-shaved skin,
And thus insult the power that first gave him

His natural mat of thermal insulation
Protective from the sun's bright scintillation, -
Or when comes down the winter's hoary frost;
Oh shall not *then* his skull deplore the loss?

Another fellow's head, both bald and big
Had been surmounted by a big brown wig.
But if you can't perceive the signs of this
Just rest assured your wignorance is bliss.

Once, long-haired louts had raised their passion
For non-shaved hair; - now razed's the fashion!
The Teds, the Neds, the Mods, the Rockers
Of one anothers' gods were mockers.

When seeing my own reflection dare I not
Imagine that the little hair I've got
Still farther from my forehead fast receding
Would ever quite respond to due re-seeding.

HAIR-RAISING COMPETITION

Whatever competition I'd be called upon
To judge, my face would sure be woe-begone
Because I'd never stand the chance at all
To be appointed to the task at all.

Both male and female, all have heads of hair
Both thick and thin, - or just no longer there.
Just look! - those lovely girls from out of school,
Not trying to look particularly cool,

Quite naturally growing their hair attractive
According to a natural directive,
Yet lending some the opportunity
To set the styles of their community

Whereby the use of strange and various gadjets
Perform hair-raising feats arranging ringlets
To run alongside thinnish strips of skin . . .
For me, thick curly locks will always win!

Thus musing, fell I fast asleep, ignoring
Those observations, now becoming boring,
But when my eyes had opened once again
They both realised as I got off the train

That my intended stop I'd passed, and thus
Arrived at journey's end, - the terminus!
A lovely lady, German and most elegant
Poured out to me her worse predicament:

She knew the language not! She'd been intending
To get to Frankfurt, - without comprehending
The train half-way she'd boarded went as far as
A well-known Frankish city known as Paris.

"I know no French, please help, I speeg a leeddle Eenglish"
"You must be hungry, would you like a little sandwich?
"Jah! Danke schön, I'm absolutely starving,"
"Now cross the platform quick, that train is leaving

For Frankfurt any moment now, - get on it!"
I grabbed her bags, and pushed her prompt upon it,
Wished her farewell in any handy language,
Then searched my bag for that tomato sandwich.

"Ah, here it is!" Stretched out my hand to give it,
But all in vain, which left us feeling livid:
Tout-d'suite the doors slid shut, the train slid out,
"Ach Scheisse!" - I distinctly heard her shout!

(PRONOUNCED "SHIEZER". AN ENGLISH EQUIVALENT EXISTS)

****

17

A TRAIN OF THOUGHT
AND THOUGHTS ABOUT ONE'S STATION

TRAVELS IN GENERAL

Should you have thought to take the train
    Then let its journey train your thought,
And should the landscape or terrain
    Be pleasing to the eye or not . . .

Surprising just how much we learn
    From human nature, largely owing
To how our leisured minds discern
    Much more than merely where we're going.

For fellow passengers converse
    As soon as one's first words are spoken;
Much information they disperse,
    The frigid ice at last being broken.

A GENERAL IN TRAVEL

For instance, one man with his wife
    Insisted I should listen to
The sordid story of his life,
    While her eyes gleamed and glistened too.

He talked about the gruesome war
    For in the army had he served,
And how his wide chest grew some more
    To hold the medals he'd deserved.

Dictators had he learnt to hate,
    Disliked obeying senseless orders,
Dared not arrive one second late
    Whenever summoned to Headquarters..

Yet duties drastic must be learnt;
    Each soldier must observe his station;
Then, rising in the ranks, he'd earned
    A wide and General education.

At giving orders he'd been hesitant,
    Full-knowing that soldiers' lives were precious.
Good men he'd seen to death being sent
    On dangerous errands too audacious.

HITLER-HATER

"Just look how Nazis forced young lads
    To do their murderous deeds with relish!
'You'll do it für das Vaterland,
    Or else by ziss machine-gun perish.'

That madman who made millions miserable
    Grown great, he gradually grew littler,
His armies once upheld him admirable,
    Till no one trusted Adolf Hitler.

His faithful followers vacillated,
    Fed-up of being dictated to!
Then planned he'd be assassinated,
    But that wise plot was fated too!

Injustice of injustice done!
    For several of his generals vanished!
By others was his war being won.
    The Führer finally being vanquished . . .

Full fearing what would happen later,
  His Frau still strangely at his side,
Gave up his rôle as Great Dictator
  By just committing suicide!

When will they learn, those crazed imposers
  Of how they wish their wicked wills
To be inflicted on most others? . . .
  And those who won't conform - one kills!

The difference 'tween us men and them"
  The General in sadness said,
"Is just that we've survived since then,
  While those poor men who died are dead."

CIVILISATION CRASHING TO A HASTY HALT?

The train went on, the topic changed,
  The General's wife would have a word in
About how peace might be arranged
  To be for all mankind rewarding.

"You see how fast this train is going!
  So smooth and so luxurious,
But have we any means of knowing
  Our end result? I'm curious!

It's somewhat different from conditions
  I once knew as a child. . . One caught
The train at various mainline stations,
  Perhaps the "Coronation Scot" . . . .

Long since run out of steam, but easily
  By diesel means and sleek design
Run twice the speed by electricity,
  So trains today take half the time."

Then adding to her theme, she spake,
    "It's from our excess speed one suffers;
Our express train without a brake . . . .
    Would sure be bound to hit the buffers!"

A CYCLIST'S LOGIC

"I'm sorry to be butting in,
    But to but-in I really must:
The brakeless train we travel in
    Just symbolises all of us.

To live on still some skill it takes,
    Which surely, Madam, you're implying?
My bicycle without its brakes
    Would also be a means of dying!

While steering clear of cars that curse us,
    We breathe their fumes that cause exhaustion,
The roads are cluttered-up; what's worse is
    We fear our cause is but a lost one!

Bring back the bus! Cut back the number
    Of private cars propelled by petrol,
By all means let our buses lumber,
    But fuelled by harmless means perpetual.

The excess cars, cut off their motors,
    Take two or three, all tailor-made
Together welded, thus promote a
    Retro-bus, as trailer-made.

Our lorries keep for distribution
    Though minus motorised resources,
But haul them by the contribution
    Of what we used to use, - strong horses.

Bring back the bike, our young ones train
    To press their pedals, making sure
They use their youthful legs again -
    An exercise most ailments cure!

Achieving this means education
    In cycle-care and maintenance.
No school-boy of whatever nation,
    Or girl, should fail to take the chance

To get to school and back by bike
    In wind or rain or hilly routes;
They'd learn to lose their fat physique,
    But keep their capes and rubber boots.

At first they will protest saying, "Ouch!" . . .
    - You're not prepared to face it, - eh? -
"More comfy is our fireside couch." . . .
    Much more conducive to obesity!

For problems of excess pollution,
    Of which us cyclists leave no trace,
The ideal ultimate solution
    Is staring at us in the face!

GENERAL ADVICE

But how, my friend, could you achieve it
    Upon this world so motorised?
Your theory's sound, as you believe it;
    Would people think your motives wise?

Harsh laws you'd have to first impose
    To bring such excess to a halt,
Because, - don't you and I suppose
    Most folk would rise up in revolt?

I sympathise with your opinion,
   But well-armed armies would be needed
Empowered with means of dread dominion
   Before your sound advice were heeded.

OUR CIVILISATION'S DOWNFALL

Although the Deutsches Autobahn
   Inspired our net of motorways
We now conclude we ought to ban
   Too many cars, find better ways . . .

Like making from their melted engines
   A thousand armoured army-tanks
To quell the crowds, - but with a vengeance
   They'd hardly give a thousand thanks!

So, let me just sum-up your theory
   In all its idealistic logic:
Of Hitler's ways mankind grew weary
   To count its consequences tragic.

I should draw up a massive list
   Retired from warfare over-done,
Though militantly pacifist,
   For shooting all who use the gun!

We're civilised! - So said the Egyptians,
   And then the Romans following Greeks.
We'd end up past all apt descriptions
   As Goths and Huns, - all nature's freaks.

The conversation gathered speed
   As did that super-speeding train
While no one guessed its brakes indeed
   Would fail, - our voyage ALL IN VAIN!

23

O'ER A' THE HILLS O' LIFE VICTORIOUS!

SOLO CYCLIST

MEDITATIONS MADE DURING A SOLO CYCLE-TRIP
TO ENGLAND, TAKING IN THE LAKE-DISTRICT.

The cyclist was a wandering boy,
   A wandering boy was he;
He'd cycled off to England
   It's foreign folks to see.

He could see   that a tree
Was as green,   that a bean
Was as tinned,   that the wind
Was as wild,   that a child
Was as young,   that a tongue
Was as long,   that a song
Was as tuneful,   that a spoonful
Was as full,   that a pool
Was as wet,   that a bet
Was as risky,   that Scots whisky
Was as popular,   that as jocular
Were the jokes,   that the folks
There who drank   would have thanked
You for filling-up   their tipple-cup,
Where stupid rhymes   they'd spin at times
Like those of Keats,   which thieving cheats
Would try to ape,   or imitate,
But minus words worth   those of Wordsworth
Who note had taken   from his Lakeland
Of Mother-Nature's   scenic features,
Describing what   he'd rightly thought
In Angle-land   were likewise grand,
Yet cyclist Stephen   felt that even
English men,   just now and then
Should draw their lots   to visit Scots
And borders cross,   to no great loss
Of integration   between each nation.

PART 2

ODD OBSERVATIONS ON ANIMALS

LONG-LEGGED BIRD

OBSERVED DURING A CYCLE-TOUR IN NORTH-GERMAN COUNTRYSIDE

One thing that still sticks in my mind and my memory
Had legs like thin sticks, and lived in North Germany,
So still did it stand that I stood there and wondered
If rather too far from its home had it wandered,
So, needing to rest for a while, it in fact
Just stood there stock-still, like a statue to act.

What breed of a bird? I just didn't know
Such knowledge so lacking I needed to owe
To someone with backing in more than mythology
But in study of birds, which we call ornithology.
Myself, being a fellow more clever with bikes,
Just calls any bird whatever one likes.

I knew that it certainly wasn't a stork,
As storks have long beaks, and this one was short,
It wasn't a heron; I'd seen such a thing go
Flap-flap as it flew; perhaps a flamingo?
No, no, it can't be, for flamingos I think
Are fowls found most frequently feathered in pink.

Of course one should never attempt to disturb
Such a deep-thinking, highly intelligent bird,
So, leaving my bicycle propped up against me
I stood just as still, as I watched it intently,
Then slowly, just slowly, one leg did it raise
The other it balanced-on midst all the maize

Which grew all around in that field where it stood;
I wondered just what it would find for its food.
Still stood on one leg, it bade me enquire
Just what was the reason behind that desire
To curl up one leg as if it were scratching
The other. And suddenly, as I kept watching,

The answer occurred as my thought-process drifted
It would fall to the ground if both had been lifted!
A worm from the earth may just pop up for breath
Unaware it would worm its way duly to death,
Then all of a sudden snapped-up by some beak
Its succulent self supplies something to eat!

A hungry big bird would be certain to so mess
Him about through the course of its digestive process.
Moreover, a blind worm with no means of knowing
Which passage he's going down, asks, "Wor'm I going?"
For such is the fate of one creature being good
For other ones, sacrificed purely for food.

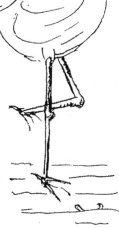

Instead, as the length of their neck big birds all-stretch
Until it resembles the neck of an ostrich,
The neck of that long-legged bird quickly twitched
For a fly had arrived just in time to be snatched
By that beak just as sharp as the bird's beady eyes
Seeing well in advance what it took by surprise.

The fly was but one of a number inside her,
The next victim could be a bee or a spider,
To keep others company till, with the worm,
To fowline nutrition they'd very soon turn.
And so the bird feasted by means rather clever
But could not continue for ever and ever.

So, standing again on two legs for an age,
The long-legged bird decided to stage
A take-off, undoubtedly destined for Dusseldorf
By flapping departure, it thereto just tootled-off,
"I'll get there before you, flying fast as I like;
You'll never keep up with me, you on your bike!"

PROBLEMS OF AN OCTOPUS
CAUGHT UP WITH HIS PROBLEMATIC OCTO-CAT

(ACKNOWLEDGEMENTS TO JOHN HEGLEY)

On the deep sandy sea-bed an opulent Octopus
    With the aid of its eight octo-tentacles
Had built for himself an eight-sided octo-house
    Each side to each-other side almost identical,
But what should be seen as no great surprise:
The octopus possessed only TWO beady eyes!

Now one of those eyes had suffered so sadly
    Because of an accident terribly tragic
His pet octo-CAT scratched one rather badly
    Which could only be righted by crafty cures magic.
That cat came in fact from far-off Saskatchewan
So each of its claws was a sharp and a scratchy one.

The eight-footed octo-puss seldom seen stockingless
    Had one furry foot for each feline sock-topus
So four pairs of socks did the pussy possess!
    But one morning early that dearly loved octopus
Was pulling his leg to try to awaken him;
The cat scratched him back attempting to shake-off him.

Espying one eye now seemingly socketless,
    The cat categorically, quite compos-mentis-ly,
Said, "Let's put to right this unseemly awful mess
    For quite obvious-lee there's sure meant-to-be
An octopus-doctor around in the sea
To care for our colony of top-octpopi!"

So off they both set by the sub-aqua bus,
    For found they around no aqua-le-copters,
Its eight octo-wheels would drive them both thus
    In hopes it would stop at the aquatic doctor's
Profoundly he'd sound them with octo-tubed stethoscope
Without which no doctor had ever success to cope.

But seeing that sad eye down-dropped from its socket
    He lost all his hope as a doctoral optimist,
"I just cannot cure this dropped-down eye-optic,
    You must go at once and visit an occulist!
But first take these pills, the purest of phosphorus,
One finds them in mines 'neath the blue sea of Bosporus.

On seeing them so deeply there bedded well down
    I realised how handy they'd come in, - essential
For octopi's eyes dropped out or dropped down.
    So let us test-out their essential potential,
They surely will cure, as never they're meant-to-kill,
Take one every hour for each octo-tenta-cle."

Thank you, we're now setting off for to see, Doctor,
    That occulist whom you've commended so.
Refreshing themselves drinking cupfuls of sea-water,
    That ultra-odd episode thus ended so:
Of which our dear octopus ever since often-talks
Of both his eyes looking so optically orthodox.

From having been hanging from one opto-socket
    Defacing his face, - what a dreadful disgrace!
Once back to its base the occulist poked it
    Now fitting so fully put back in its place.
That eye, very nearly being an-eye-hilated,
Since then kept its keeper so highly elated!

Whatever the hardships which oft-times beset
    An octopus having such problems so optic,
He ought to reflect whenever upset
    That traumas or tragedies, - a typical topic!
Pr'aps caused by one's octo-cat often can be
Ascribed to conditions of cat-astro-phee!

THE REBELLIOUS SHEEP

ON RECEIVING A POST-CARD PORTRAYING
A FLOCK OF SHEEP BEING HERDED
OBEDIENTLY BY A TRIO OF SHEEP-DOGS.
BUT ONE INDEPENDENT-MINDED SHEEP WAS
DEFIANTLY PROCEEDING IN QUITE ANOTHER
DIRECTION, TO THE ANNOYANCE OF THOSE
WOOFING DOGS SAYING, "THERE'S ALWAYS
ONE ISN'T THERE? DAMNED INDIVIDUALIST!"

On every sheep there hangs a tail
    More probably a moral,
Whichever tells the truer tale,
    About which let's not quarrel.

As souvenir that card I'll keep.
    And guard its sound advice:-
All out of step those silly sheep
    Who think of nothing twice

Apart from one who'd never heard
    In his enlightened view
Of following the common herd;
    His own path to pursue!

It takes all types to make such flocks
    Of varying stupidity
But be beware of barking dogs
    Who try to curb your liberty;

By all means let them bark away
    So long as they don't bite,
For individuals mark a way
    To exercise their right.

Keep up your tail, don't let it sag!
  Do not capitulate
To dog-matism! Let it wag,
  And don't give in to fate,

For far from free upon their trotters
  In herds of much monotony,
Those "moutons" end up on our platters
  As mutton for our gluttony.

SAD STORY of the SPIDER
(I'D SPIED HER DURING A STAY IN EAST GERMANY)

We hardly can put-off until our "manjanas"
The task of putting on night-worn pyjamas.
But one thought occurred: I should surely regret a lot
Just leaving my house-floor all covered in grit and grot.

So why not make use of that old brush and shovel
Which hung from a hook in that old Prussian hovel
Instead of being lazy and leaving unswept
The floor of my shack? - For I once was adept . . .

At sweeping the streets, so why not just go for
The less tiresome task of vacating the sofa?
Too long had that broom from its hook hung around;
A task for its talents must surely be found!

The moment I reached out in order to grab it
Were such sweeping changes being made to its habit
Whereby dusty floor-boards a few moments on
Became duly dustless, and dustlessly shone!

But something just happened then, - most detrimentally, -
The broom brushed a SPIDER, though quite accidentally!
Its body un-injured and mainly un-mangled . . .
But look at its long legs, so badly entangled!

Those spidery limbs seem deceptively fragile
For walking up walls, seen on ceilings so agile,
On eight legs they crawl around, not simply six,
But damage to one of them, - how does one fix?

Just how can first-aiders propose to put right
Such problems so painfully posed to their plight?
They stand or they fall upon their last legs,
But can one replace them with false wooden pegs?

No future I saw for her, - turned to her past, -
At swinging from ceilings she seemed unsurpassed
While spinning long yarns from her inermost coils
Each masterpiece making by such self-skilled toils,

Which people perceptive most readily will agree
Are fashioned in form from finest-spun filigree,
Thenceforth she'd ensure that she watchfully kept sight
Of how she'd so wondrously woven her web-site.

Being no vegetarian, she'd watch from some angle
In wait for what meat she could catch in its tangle,
But now were her days, like her legs, sadly numbered
I'd sure be amazed if she'd last while I slumbered.

So, lifting her poor crippled self to my window-sill,
Now placed on a pad in hopes she was living still,
I'd doubted a doctor would have the success to cope
With hearing no heart-beat by means of his stethoscope.

One last look I took before going to bed,
But sadly the spider already was dead!
Refraining from further and fruitless floor-sweeping,
I dreamt of her sad fate while un-sweetly sleeping.

MOUSTERPIECE of DISCOVERY
INSTALLING SOME PLUMBING-PIPES IN AN ANCIENT GERMAN
HOUSE, WE HAD TO OPEN UP A SECTION OF STAIRCASE FOR ACCESS.
ONE NEVER KNOWS WHAT ONE MAY FIND!

While working in our upper storey
    We found remains of what appeared
To tell its own historic story:-
    A MOUSE her family had reared
Between two treads within the staircase
    Where she could safely build her mouse-nest
For there at last she'd found a spare space.
    How undeserved the name of house-pest!

Or was it Father-mouse who'd built it?
    Just bit by bit or phase by phase,
While Mother-mouse by instinct filled it
    Quite out of sight from human gaze
With what we may regard as oddities
    But which as mother she knew best
As needful family commodities
    For furnishing their own new nest?

We'd given that site a good hard stare,
    Surveyed it highly interested,
Surprised to find that hardwood stair
    Had one time been by mice infested!
Amongst the stubble, empty shells
    Of hazel-nuts, strange things they'd chewed,
A single sign showed up that tells
    That for their intellectual food

They read newspapers on occasion,
  Folk lacking sense leave lying around,
Then tear them up as insulation.
  To back this evidence was found:
One scrap of script and what was writ on it
  Beyond all doubt bade us determine
That mice are by no means illiterate.
  That blatt in fact was writ in German!

Now should a mouse end up as houseless
  It may discern twixt caves and cages,
Or just proceed to build its mouse-nest
  Quite unconcerned about mort-gages,
Importing from the world exterior
  Materials varied, miscellaneous,
Then sports its way into th'interior,
  Such modes being known as mouse-hole-aneous!

Now folk, - we fill with food our fridges
  For feeding growing girls and boys on,
Just think how mice will justly judge us
  For forcing them to feed on poison!
They're neither dull nor daft nor dense, -
  Chew literature between each meal, -
As those small scraps of evidence
  Incontrovertibly reveal.

DEAR MOUSE, - YOU'VE LONG SINCE MET YOUR TERMINUS
OUR HOUSE, THANK YOU, YOU'VE LEFT NON-VERMINOUS!

37

HOW HORSES HOB-NOBBED IN HILLHEAD

HOW HORSES of HILLHEAD
KEPT HOB-NOBBING

Horses who hailed from Hillhead and nearby Kelvinside,
districts of Glasgow's West-end, preferred being entirely
untethered by rules of grammar, punctuation, or spelling.

Two fine handsome horses once happened to meet
At the corner of Hillhead and steep Great George Street.
   One grey mare called Whinnie,
     Black Pete being the other;
   They didn't get many
     Such chances to blether.

The drivers had left them to stand for ten minutes
While attending the needs of householders and tenants.
   Withdrawing their noses
     From bags full of fodder,
   Told tales one supposes
     Could hardly be odder,

Pete prattling on about how a horse maddens
When constantly carrying coals from Cowcaddens.
   It's worse when it's hilly
     Like Hillhead and such,
   This place wid sure kill ye!
     I don't like it much.

My driver is dirty; all coated in black,
Poor devil! He humphs heavy bags on his back.
   A thick pad with studs on
     Keeps coal-bags from chaffin
   His back by his burden, -
     Neigh matter fur laffin'!

What's worse, he went on as he warmed to his theme,
That coal simply sends so much soot on the scene,
    As people just burn it
      Who dwell in this zone,
    To smoke simply turn it,
      Hence spoil the ozone!

Now Whinnie was much mare 'refained' as a carrier;
As '*de*-stinked' from Pete, that mare was the merrier.
    Whereas Peat would sweat,
      She simply perspired,
    Yet held no regret
      For thus was she hired:

To encourage a carriage from Bill Beattie's Bakery
And cope with those cobble-stones shoogily and shakily
    Delivering big batches
      Of bread, - plain, pan, wheaten,
    Through retailers' hatches,
      First purchased, then eaten.

But Och! said she, shaking the hair of her main,
It's hard work to drag carts and climb this 'inclain'
    Great George Street, said she,
      Is too steep and hilly,
    And no place for me
      Not long since a filly.

Now Pete in his sympathy pressed his mute muzzle
Upon that of Whinnie, most fondly to nuzzle,
    Suggesting a date,
      Tonight? Feeling lax?
    We might even mate
      Once rid of those sax!

Now 'sax' had a meaning which she had mistaken
As being rather 'risqué', yet fun lightly taken,
 Some thought 'sex' were 'begs'
  With coal stecked insaid, -
 Or so said 'old hegs'
  Who haunt Kelvinsaid.

Their quaint conversation was curtly cut short.
Their reins being resumed, they presumed with a snort
 Meant trotting Dowanhill-wards
  Against brakes applied
 Where drivers played billiards
  Unseen once inside.

But on the way down, a shoe had come loose,
Which made a strange sound on Whinnie's hard hooves.
 No billiards for Bill
  Her driver, but worst-of-all,
 He'd have to fulfil
  A visit to 'horspital'.

This meant that poor Whinnie must limp to some stable
To find some bold blacksmith, both burly and able.
 There's one in Otago Street
  Or was only yesterday
 So that's were I *may* go, Pete,
  I'll hoof it there anyway.

And sure enough, opposite Cowan Street, an archway
Led horses and mares direct to auld Archie
 Who, though deaf and dumb,
  Had hands deft and dextrous;
 To him they'd succumb,
  Fore-legs ambidextrous,

"A CHANGE FROM CONSTANT CORN & HUSKS
THOSE HUBBARD'S CELEBRATED RUSKS!"

For knowing how to handle a horse, how to please,
He'd soothe them with sugar-lumps, put each at ease,
 While huge nails he heated
 Till more than red-hot
 Then hammer them, seated
 In just the right spot.

The horses enjoyed this brief break from monotony,
He'd cereally feed them on oats when he'd got any.
 They'd thank him, revealing
 With grateful short snorts,
 He'd just the right feeling
 For legs (of *their* sorts)!

So shod with her new shoe, the latest steel issue,
Being horse-shoe in shape, good-luck would it wish you,
 Dear Whin in smart livery
 To Hubbards proceeded
 Where, on each delivery,
 On stale rusks she feeded.

Now, quite by co-incidence, who else had arrived
At that self-same kerbside but Pete who'd survived
 The pains and the aches
 That quite a long haul
 Inflicted, with brakes
 Pulled on going downhill.

Ah Whinnie! he whinnied, - We meet once again!
Tonight, don't you think, you could loosen your rein?
 I'll show you our bridal-suite,
 Have *no* nuptial fears!
 Said Win, Hold the bridle, Pete,
 Or just hold my ears!

So later that evening being free and being able
They met in a field well away from their stable.
　　Though each had been tied
　　Secure by a rope,
　　They'd chewed through and tried
　　To quietly elope.

Now what happened next one must merely imagine,
Though one might expect that their time was neigh bad yin.
　　With After-Eight-Mints
　　After foaling around,
　　In eight-and-three minths
　　A new foal was found.

He grew to compare with his Père and his Mère,
But sadly was work found for horse-power nae mare.
　　Being over-abundant
　　Too many were shod.
　　Beheld as redundant,
　　That poor foal was shot!

Neither horse nor the mare was accorded due honour,
Instead, heavy loads were laid on him and on her.
　　Replaced by the lorry
　　By petrol propelled,
　　For horses we're sorry
　　Reins no more are held!

Note:　In the days of horse-drawn transport, it was not
　　　only coal-carts and bread-vans that were drawn,
　　　but also trams, hansome-cabs, hearses, fire-engines,
　　　delivery-vans. The horses were often teamed in twos
　　　or even fours according to need. Horse-flesh during
　　　the war-time years was available not only for animal
　　　consumption!

LET'S HAVE A LEISURELY LOOK AT LITTLE LIZARDS
(A RECOLLECTION ADDRESSED TO CHILDREN)

Down by the riverside one day,
    A day so warm and sunny,
Small creatures had come out to play
    Their antics highly funny, '
    Should one dare venture near?

Around the rocks they run for fun,
    They love the weather hot and dry,
But seeing a stranger, - off they run!
    You don't get time to ask them why,
    They simply disappear!

Upon a shiny rock at whiles
    One waits, - a sun-warmed rock and smooth, -
To see those tiny crocodiles
    Creep out from crevice, crack, or groove.
    One must not budge an inch!

Ah! There go two intrepid ceatures
    So smartly dressed morocco-style
All tailor-made to match such features
    Befitting best a crocodile:-
    Long snouts, long tails that swish,

Four legs equipped with claws like fingers
    To grip that rocky face while scurrying,
For sure a lizard never lingers
    But darts around at high-speed hurrying
    To find some tasty food.

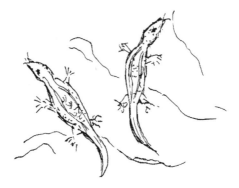

There! Creeping out from cracks and crevices
    They catch such fleas, or flies, or ants
As run the risk. - Served up for breakfast is
    The fate they face, and stand no chance
    Apart from tasting good!

Forked tongues flick out to quickly catch them;
    The lizards lick their lips with relish!
What happens next one can't imagine
    Except the process must be hellish, -
    A diabolic festival!

Two lizards stopped quite suddenly
    Each thinking me a stony statue,
One spoke, as he just turned to me
    To introduce himself as MATTHEW.
    Next thing he said was best-of-all:

His favourite mate, his female lizard,
    Was named to suit a lizard best,
For both her parents had considered
    To call the lass E-LIZARD-BETH,
    Which suits her fine, I guess.

Just then, I had to move, - as ants
    Had occupied that spot a while
To feast on fleas found in my pants,
    Their bites as bad's a crocodile
    Who'd snap up human flesh!

DISREPUTABLE REPTILES

CREATURES CALLED CROCODILES
TOO RISKY FOR TOURISTS TO TAKE CLOSE-UP SNAPS OF!

Should distant New Zealand be your destination,
Come back to your homeland with true information
Concerning those creatures called crocodiles, crawling
Round banks of the riverside hoping you'd fall in
Or slide down the slime in a split-second reckless;
They'd reckon it's time you were beckoned for breakfast!

Of reptiles like these do we hear scary tales!
At the opposite end from their rear scaly tails
Such hazards they have in those snap-happy snouts
About which you'd hardly have slap-happy doubts,
With the power to devour by their cool capability
Whoever falls foul of such cruel snapability.

So don't get too close-up when taking your snaps!
A single sharp snap from one of those chaps
Could leave you being bodily bit in duality,
And instantly left with a split personality!
That reptile with eyes-closed, apparently napping,
Lies waiting in hopes it is *you* he's caught napping.

New-Zealand itself where visitors stop a while
Was cut clean in two by a vicious old crocodile,
Or so it is claimed by a time-honoured legend,
And thus has remained, and not merely imagined.
Think! - Next time you order your crocodile-steaks,
Try not to make fatally awful mistakes.

Recall that your hand-bag of easy convenience
Is crocodile skin, while, crying out for vengeance,
His next-of-skin, motionless, waits by the river,
Looks just like a log of no danger whatever,
But should you intrepidly tread on its bark,
Be DEAD-sure his teeth are incredibly sharp!

KATRINA'S CAT

Already, much excess is written
Concerning countless cats and kittens,
So to the reader's great relief
We'll keep these comments strictly brief:

Katrina's cat did intermittently
Have kittens in her litter, didn't she?
And played her part full-willingly
Conceiving kittens most fulfillingly,

By father-cat infatuated,
That further cats be procreated,
Submitting to his will admittedly,
She let him play his part unstintingly!

Well-practised in such voluntary acts.
In course of time a colony of cats
Came into being, - quite unbelievable,
That kittens could be inconceivable!

BEE RESCUED - from drowning

What be this creature lying in that puddle
Upon its back, and in a hapless struggle?
For insects in an upside-down position
Can rarely right themselves by intuition,
And thus they beg some human understanding
Until upon their legs again they're standing.

Upon their legs . . . but what about their wings
When simply sodden, - limply useless things?
So drenched and drooping, would they fly again?
All efforts to restore them would seem quite in vain.
Meanwhile those spindly legs like flails were beating
To sky up-raised, for urgent aid entreating.

Ah, - found a fiver! - pulled it from my pocket,
It's just the thing, I thought, on which to prop it.
While still her fragile frantic limbs she waved,
Arrives at last first-aid to have her saved!
That five-pound note conveyed her to a deck-chair
Where she could dry-out in the sun just left there.

Though patience be a virtue, time for healing
Needs backing-up by sympathetic feeling.
As still she lay, a half-drowned drookit object
I wondered if she would survive in state so abject.
Yet if the poor thing feels a need for food,
A little honey might just do her good!

For, as she'd always been a busy BEE,
To her own produce she'd entitled be,
From lavender, from rose, from hollihock,
Such provender she'd hold the lot in stock
Now safely stored within her busy hive.
One drop may she require to keep alive?

So setting down a spot of golden honey,
(The stuff that's stiff, and not the stuff that's runny),
I watched and waited, - no need to direct her!
Her instincts prompted her to feed on nectar.
Inevitably, soon and sure enough,
Her tongue stretched-out to suck the sticky stuff.

From being immobile, shortly she revived!!!
That miracle from honey thus supplied
Had worked its wonders, need one wonder why?
Would she, one wondered, learn once more to fly?
Once more she walked on legs, at first unsteady,
Then shook her sodden wings till dry, - now ready

To buzz-off, to her rescuer's delight,
Not far off, - self-propelled in flight, -
To work without the slightest hesitation
Amongst the floral fields of her profession
Which means, before those flowery blooms have fallen
She'd centri-petally remove their pollen.

One doubts if mere mankind can ever be
As efficacious as that clever bee.
At flight adept, no helicopter can
Compete, being just designed and made by man,
Yet unkind criticism's indefensible;
For rescuing, 'copters sure are indispensible.

The bee possesses, true, her painful sting,
For self-defence can be a gainful thing.
While cats can scratch, and dogs can badly bite,
And boys to fight with flying fists delight.
Yet, should a bumble-bee in trouble be,
Supply some succour to that humble bee.

If ever called upon to be its saviour
Commended shall ye be for your bee-haviour.

A STAR ATTRACTION

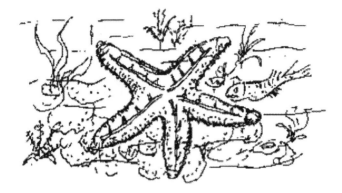

Although a star-attraction,
    Officially those STARFISH,
Of fishy forms a faction,
    (If actually they *are* fish),
Are known by their inaction
    So lie flat when they wish.

Big fish who wish to swallow them
    Will soon feel disappointed
Disorders sure will follow when
    Digestion gets disjointed
For little knowledge do they ken
    Of starfish, all five-pointed.

Each pointed arm has pointed prickles
    Emitting venom vile
So from that star that more than tickles
    A fish should swim a mile,
And even sharks should shun that quality
    That could affect their poisonality.

PART 3

IN TRIBUTE TO OUR TRADESMEN

JACK JOHNSTON THE JOINER

You'd visit Jack Johnston on business, or chat
While scrounging some sawdust required for your cat,
The sawdust you'd spread with great care on a tray
Whereon the cat creeps and then craps day by day.

Jack's brains you may pick, but he'd answer most modest
"Ye'll find them o'er there in thae bags o' sawdust."
It fell from his bench in the centre of which
A multi-toothed wheel, at the touch of a switch

Would suddenly spring into swift swish, swish, swishing,
Then cut planks in strips with perfect precision
At ten times the speed of an ordinary hand-saw.
He'd then feel the need to switch-on his band-saw.

For objects devised and designed on the drawing-board
Await being realised and consigned to his sawing-board.
Large logs which had long lay aloft in his loft would
Be brought down, transformed, whether hardwood or
softwood,

Into cabinets, window-frames, doors glazed or plain,
So shaped by Jack's chisel, sure-shaved by his plane,
All worked with such accurate skill, and much pride,
But just take a look at the place from outside!

As shoes of the cobbler's bairns tend to be tattered,
Just so was the joiner's shed, looking half-shattered!
For rain-drops came down from his roof free-admitted,
As drafts crept through doorways and windows ill-fitted.

Just too taken-up with the comfort of clients
To think of his own, Jack just suffered in silence,
Intent on employing his powers of perception
Creating his works-of-fine-art to perfection.

OLD PAUL THE PLUMBER

The PLUMBER, old Paul, had a workshop mid-town;
Pipes stood-up in stock, to eventually drain down, -
He'd fat ones, six-inchers, four-inchers, slim copper ones,
Old drawers to hold various objects, all proper ones,
Divided in squares holding couplings and branches,
Brand new, not exposed yet to unpleasant stenches

Which plumbers conditioned to skilled diagnosis
Distinguish by sniffing through highly-trained noses
Old Paul by our own nose we'd sense right away
For hung from his mouth was a pipe made of clay,
Its stem held a miniature W.C.
Which caused to his clients much trouble, you see,

For into that bowl would he stuff shreds of shag
He constantly kept in a small leather bag,
The shag he would light till that red-glowing stuff
Was sucked-in as smoke, blown-out by Paul's puff.
He spoke with authority, soundly rehearsed
In causes of blockages, leaks, or pipes burst,

As happens mid-winter, when other folks normally
Are seated at table, prepared to dine formally,
Or lounging at leisure, their firesides around,
In dream-lands of pleasure, - till some SNAG is found
Upsetting their comfort by some cause uncommon
Creating some crisis, then . . . whom do they summon?

Of course it is Paul the old Plumber, - no matter
His hot Christmas dinner's growing cold on his platter,
He lays down his knife, his fork, and his spoon,
Assures you he's just on his way, - will come soon!
Arriving, he looks round, pronounces his verdict,
"Your plumbing I've found to be worse than imperfect."

"Your drain-pipe outside has long since been choked."
(We also were choked by the pipe that Paul smoked.)
"And that's why your W.C.-level's rising
You put down too much; it's hardly surprising!
Connections ill-fitted, and that's no the worst;
Inspection will tell ye some auld yins are burst."

His big bag of gadjets and spanners and spares
He fetches from back of his van for repairs,
Has everything done in half-hour or less
Leaves nothing behind, he's cleared up the mess.
Late back to his dinner, his wife grown accustomed
To heating his cold Christmas pudding and custard,

The telephone rings again, Paul must emerge and see
If he can attend to another emergency!
There's only one man in the town who is sure
Of where every drain diverts into which sewer;
Kens every turn taken its contents to pass,
And sees though thick soil as if it were glass!

For pipes must conduct in this affluent new-age
Those unwanted products of effluent sewage.
For folk, as they flush well-away from their territory,
Ken fine that they don't want it kept for posterity.
Though Paul was a personage quite indispensable,
Who served us all well by a work-load immeasurable,

A life-time of toil left his back bent quite badly
Now gone from our soil, we all miss him sadly.
No longer his dense clouds of smoke can we sniff;
His soul now exudes a more sweet-scented whiff
Where Paul need not bother with down-pipes or rhones
Perfection's pipes play in those far smokeless zones.

Our problems he solved, though we saw them but sordidly,
Deserves he due recompense, paying him rewardedly,
As lives on his soul, plus his wisdom and wit,
It's only Paul's body lies buried in SH-ingle.

BIG BRIAN the BLACKSMITH

It took B-B-BRIAN to handle the hammer
That bounced up and down in time with his stammer;
It clanged and it clinked with a regular ring
To turn-out from straight lengths of steel, anything
From circular scrolls, so graceful in form,
To whatever mould made its function perform
For whatever purpose, already defined
By some deft designer, creative in mind.

You name it, he'd make it, contriving new features
Un-dreamt-of before by less clever creatures:
From wrought-iron hand-railings, and hinged ornate gates
Staircases with thick treads of steel chequer-plates,
"Harmonious Blacksmith" as scribed by George Handel *
Was much more percussive when Brian would handle
His dinging and donging with hard "Heavy Metal",
Well tuned-in with musical ears in fine fettle. (* composition of
that name)

Ah! - this was his music of making in steel
Such objects ironically useful and real.
While working away at his forge he would never
Lay down for an instant his tools, - for whoever
Might try to engage him in trite conversation
Would just have to wait until Brian's concentration
Died-down, like the furnace he'd blown by its bellows
Once white-hot, now mellowed to bright reds and yellows.

He could be mistaken for Satan when such works
Had he undertaken, like forging-out pitch-forks,
His eyes looked like Lucifer's lit-up by flame,
Yet melting from wildness to mildness more tame,
As, once more relaxed, he would graciously turn his
Attentions to **YOU**, and his back on his furnace,
Acknowledge your presence, accomplished his task,
And "G-G-Guid-day, sir! How are ye?" he'd ask.

Once B-B-Big Brian had you civilly greeted,
His words would be poured-out, and often repeated,
Repeated, repeated, repeated, repeated.

DANIEL THE DIGGER-DRIVER
(Normally known by nickname as 'Big Digger')

Dear Daniel Delaney who drove the big-digger
    Arrived first on site,
For there he'd be, starting at eight; - one would figure
    He'd finish that night, -
Which turned-out good news, for things were on schedule,
    They'd started on time!
What's more he would work with a movement perpetual
    His skill quite in line . . .

With all the precision with which he would wield
    That powerful machine,
Controlling each move, as it dug up that field
    As master supreme!
For Daniel Delaney, a gem of a man,
    Was highly reliable
For every consignment that anyone ran
    Turned out highly viable.

His digger would root out large rocks from the soil,
    Move mountains of mud,
Then smooth the site over, with versatile toil,
    Round deep ditches dug.
Next morning's delivery, scheduled by lorry,
    Of 'Ready-Mix' concrete
Would fill Daniel's ditches with porridge-like slurry
    From all it could ex-crete,

While Dan would advance good advice and sound guidance,
    The tricks of his trade,
Where concrete foundations would face no subsidence,
    Where drains should be laid.

Of good men like Daniel our world is the richer,
    Of whom we feel proud,
Few portraits are painted, portrayed in some picture,
    Nor broadcast aloud,

But, matching their modest demeanour so passive
    And honest good-will,
They've masterly modes of manoevring massive
    Machines by their skill.
Each evening Dan's elbow gets bent in the bar,
    A glass in his hand;
His cronies have gathered from near and from far
    A convivial band.

They chat in the 'local' with friendly debate
    The day's deeds discuss, -
Which team will be winning on Saturday's date,
    Which loser's forecast.
Precisely the purpose that taverns are for:-
    Where men can unwind,
Opinions compare, and over a jar
    Say what's in their mind.

The various trades come together as one
    To put the world right,
In each other's company blether they on
    Till latish each night.
The world that they represent, - saints and the sane,
    Compare their experience;
Next day they'll return to their toils and their strain,
    Now no longer weary ones.

When all types of trades and all tradesmen together
    Agree how immense is
The debt that they're due to Dan the 'Big Digger',
    United concensus!

BILL THE BUILDER
AND HIS BUDDIES

BEFORE THE BUILDING BEGINS

A building, irrespective of its purpose,
Must first have gathered, most essential,
A team of tradesmen all constructive
Together with combined potential

For working under, - guess just whom?
Not only versed in work of clerks,
One first-rate builder, we assume!
Experienced as Clerk of Works

That Builder-Boy well-known as Bill . . .
Not only knew full-well his trade,
A complex rôle need he fulfill . . .
Much more than just how bricks are laid,

Knew how to read all plans previsioned
By Archibald the Architect;
With geometrical precision,
Marked out whereon the land be set . . .

The building at its every level
By instruments they a' delight
To tri-pod, standing on the gravel,
Such as the old theodolite.

Marked-out by tent-pegs stretching strings;
Set-squares inspired by old Pythagoras
Keep angles right when measuring things
His geo-metry at the back of us.

THE TEAM GETS TOGETHER

The concrete laid by Dan Delaney
Now hard, and seeming strongly set,
Despite the recent weather rainy,
Together as a team they met.

Old Paul the Plumber knew exactly
Just where his pipes of P.V.C.
Must be connected-up directly
And where all gutter-pipes should be.

Ah - welcome! Have we in addition,
Another tradesman just as valuable,
Young Ernest Ellis, electrician,
Equipped with countless cables coilable.

Here comes the Joiner known as Jack,
Jack Johnston, famed so well by name,
Complete with hammer to attack
The task of knocking-up the frame.

"You've come too soon that task to face
We're not quite ready for you yet;
Come back when we have built the base,
Once our cement's no longer wet."

So off strolled Jack the fabricator
Along to his old mini-factory
To make his frame, then pack it later
With insulation satisfactory.

The Brickie'd left a gap enabling
The meter-box to be be emplaced.
Arriving prompt to fit the cabling
The "Sparky" back to site had raced.

THE PROJECT PROCEEDS APACE

The flooring-joists that Jack had placed
All equal-spaced, but not too widely,
For Ernie Ellis, ever braced
To slip between, being thin and wiry.

He got wired-in the very date
And all that day worked steady,
But plugs and sockets had to wait
Until the plaster-board was ready.

All so exciting, much in motion,
Progressing perfectly to schedule,
External walls being built with caution,
For Mark the Mason used his noddle.

By faith, no Freemason was he
But weighed his work with every stone
So never was his masonry free
He'd charge his stonework by the ton!

Meanwhile the raftered roof in skeleton,
Awaited due attention later,
Would soon be planked, black felt upon,
Then slated by Sam Smith the Slater,

By which time Paul the Plumber came
To spend his long productive hours,
En-closet-ed, knowing well his game,
With wash-hand-basins, baths, and showers,

The electrician from above
At last disclosed the gladsome news,
His right hand in a rubber glove,
"All's well! No need to blow a fuse."

COUNT-DOWN TO COMPLETION

The fireplace, useful thing in winter,
As built by Mark, - a useful bloke,
Drew well, with not a single hint'o
Internally escaping smoke.

Big Brain unfailingly arrived
To set in place his splendid series
Of wought-iron railings he'd devised
Adorned with scrolls and whigmaleeries.

A glazed expression on his face,
The joiner came to glaze the windows.
Now don't forget the plasterer, please,
Who works as fast as any wind blows.

Now, soon or late, you might expect a
Visit from Inspector Hector
The dreaded Building-Works Inspector
Equipped with his defects-detector.

He'd come at frequent intervals,
But luckily, and most convenient,
His final visit found no faults
At last being in a mood more lenient.

Arrived back from the carpet-market,
The proud Proprietor plus his wife
Agreed Completion-Day they'd mark it
The date most joyous of their life!

"Congratulations, friends, contractors!
All thanks to you, we're moving in.
Our lovely house you've made in fact is
No mere machine for living in!"

THE MAN THAT WAS MISSING
HAS ARCHIBALD THE ARCHITECT ARRIVED?

Now, what was that you called the house we built?
    You said it's just "a living-in machine"!
Now lest that limited idea be felt
    To adequately describe the scene,
Let's drop into a drowsy world of dream: . . .

Arrayed around the building-site were men
    Who seemed all set for tackling the task
Been summoned to arrive at ten-to-ten,
    Each one of them a question had to ask,
Each question asked was virtually the same.

But wait! Here comes the owner of the site
    As sold through Sandy the Solicitor
He's here to tell us what he wants; - he might
    As well have come along as visitor.
He thinks he kens it all, but seldom right!

"Eoh, Yass! I want the entrance-doah just hya,
    The living-room I want to face the sun.
You might as well just put the staircase thyah
    I tell you, once the weuk you hyave begun,
Just carry on, I'll pay you awl next yaah."

So on he raved, as faces fell and frowned;
    Then Digger, Dan, indignantly departed
Big Bill the builder spat upon the ground
    Jack Johnston, joiner, looked the more-disjointed.
They one by one stalked off. - No one around?

But just before they all had gone away,
The question everyone had raised together
Arose as if it meant to stick and stay,
For no one present had disputed ever
That Archibald should really have his say,

Site-owner Owen thought he could dispense,
In most misguided crass naïvity,
With service, indispensably immense,
Of Archibald whose creativity
He'd reckoned as unneccessary expense!

Now Archibald had studied every aspect
Of building-skills both old and up-to-date,
Not only as designer-architect
But one who also could co-ordinate
A team of various tradesmen who'd expect

That he'd present his plans as top-priority
Before a single soul could start on site,
For some one must in seniority
Be leader of that team ere they'd unite
Beneath his well-informed authority.

Each aspect of the project shown on plans
Submitted to the Council for approval
He'd scrupulously thought-out in advance,
Sent out for several estimates, - above all
Gave every member of that team fair chance

To come together as a team creative,
Creating works of wonder with ability
With prime-creator there so they could make it. -
No claim had Archibald to God's divinity,
But took a modest pride in his humility!

A PERSPICACIOUS PEEP
INTO A STAINED-GLASS
WORKSHOP

On discovering the existence of a busy WORKSHOP
where STAINED GLASS ARTISTS still perpetuate
an ancient craft in ways that have but little changed
in centuries, one had emerged singing its praises to a
well-known German hymn-tune called "Wir Pflügen"
of which the refrain is marked below. (*) Try it!

The field of ART's well scattered
    With craftsmen of all kinds,
But one that's mainly mattered
    To perspicacious minds
Has left them much enlightened
    By richly coloured views
As seen through windows brightened
    In gorgeous tones and hues.

*   All good glass around us
    Thus lit from light above,
    Is such one should show gratitude
    For labours of much love.

No glazier's reputation
    Can stand adversely stained
For in each installation
    He places panels paned
In glass of glorious colours
    All rich in radiant light
And infinitely various
    Produced in patterns bright.

For specialists efficient
In this most ancient art
No special list's sufficient
To praise them, poles apart
From ordinary glaziers
Whose craft is far surpassed
By those whose task's not easier
And has them all outclassed.

****

A drawing first is drafted
On cardboard white and stiff
Then bits of glass are crafted
To cover it all with
Appropriate panels sitting
Each in its proper place
And cut to size for fitting
The function it must face.

Upon each fragment's surface,
The picture to complete
Where detail not enough is,
Thin lines are painted neat.
Then all apart dismembered
A kiln those bits will bake
Before being re-assembled
Now permanised that paint.

With patient care proceeding,
Around these shapes are led
Such borders as they're needing
In H-shaped strips of lead.
All joints are joined with solder,
Then by a secret ruse,
The glazing now grown colder
Is rendered waterproof.

Big bars to banish bending
At intervals are placed.
Great strength are these now lending
Against wind-pressure braced
Ensuring sun in summer
Will neither warp nor wilt
Such works of artful wonder
So beautifully built.

For centuries, six or seven,
Have windows so sublime
Been pointing up to heaven
To symbolise its clime.
Such scenes in settings splendid
Stand unsurpassed in Chartres.
And yet be it remembered
Time-honoured rest these arts!

To heighten light's rich assets,
Stained-glass may still be found
In multifarious facets
With lead-work wrapped around.
Avoiding imitations,
Despising P.V.C.,
Those craftsmanlike creations
Are wonderful to see.

MICHAEL'S CYCLE SHOP

It was only a skip and a jump and a hop
    To get to the bicycle-shop known as Michael's;
For sale in that highly accessible shop
    Was every accessory necessary for cycles.

We had him geared-up with the nick-name of Sturmey,
    Arriving, we'd hail him thus till our departure
Although his career was more placid than stormy.
    Those gears were well-known by the name "Sturmey-Archer"

About which a little non-technical chatter
    Need not be unduly excessive, one feels,
To help us arrive at the hub of the matter
    For hubs have been always essential to wheels.

They functioned, those hub-gears, with small slender springs
    Like clockwork, devised to activate ratchets,
But should they give up in despair, then those things
    Would fail in their function each ratchet to catch it.

So cleverly hidden, those gears in their hubs
    Just sometimes subjected the cyclist to failure,
Being somewhat despised by those cycling in clubs
    Preferring those external gears called 'derailleur'.

Derailleurs can also give problems, you must
    Avoid chain-reactions; clean out all that muck,
Free cog-wheels from rust, take care to adjust,
    Or else your chain's action will surely get stuck.

Now after much changing throughout many years
    We've gradually adapted to Japanese design, . . .
Slick systems devised to change cyclist's gears
    And give to the cyclist chap-an-easy time.

Both external gears and hub-gears evolve
    Much credit being due to Mr Shimano,
With passing of years, while wheels still revolve,
    So old Michael's grandson, ah! - now he's your man, oh!

Mike also built wheels with the skill of a harpist
    Except it was spokes and not strings that he strummed;
He knew where to put their blunt ends and the sharpest
    In whatever wheel by his skilled hands he turned.

The blunt ends of spokes into hub-holes inserted
    Their sharp ends he'd poke through those holes in the rim,
Same number of holes, he'd verificated, -
    A job just a little bit boring for him!

A front wheel is simpler to build than a rear-wheel,
    For one side's the same as the other side, actually,
No need for that chain-driven wheel or the gear-wheel;
    It simply revolves round its hub, turning axially.

A spokesman for spokes knows they do not just radiate
    But cross one another to add to their strength,
Moreover, those spokes for the rear-wheels must variate
    Each side having spokes of a disparate length!

To make a slight study of relevant facts will,
    As one turns one's mind to deep cogitating,
Reveal that just one end of the rear-wheel's back axle
    Accommodates sprockets with steel cogs rotating.

So two sets of spokes set-aside as selected
    Ensure that the cog-wheel's correctly positioned
Each spoke-size to left or to right side directed
    As Michael so rightly had wisely pre-visioned.

Though wheels are mankind's original invention
    Turned out not in nature's own factories,
They still keep on turning, as by revolution
    They've long since assisted in mankind's trajectories.

And yet by themselves they have little impact
    Unless by a functional frame held in place
Plus pedals providing propulsion in fact
    While handlebars steer to the end of the race.

The saddle one sits upon, - no need to mention;
    To slow down the journey, one pulls on the brakes,
Ensure that you make it your earnest intention
    To keep them adjusted, great care as one takes.

The bikes known as "Raleigh" were all made in Nottingham
    As Michael would surely declare in bold voice,
I hesitate not in selling or stocking them,
    Of bicycles truly are they the 'Rolls-Royce'!

Two models, the 'Roadster' and 'Sports', on display,
    Their 'Dyno-Hubs' turning out real car-type lighting!
But rather too heavy for people today;
    For much lighter bicycles cyclists kept fighting.

We now have our bicycles light-weight in plenty
    Beneficial for fresh-air and exercise,
So cyclists enlightened with heads far from empty
    Such benefits freely will sure recognise.

One fact that we sadly must all face today:
    Our constant confinement within cars' interiors
Contributes disgracefully to grossest obesity
    Developing excessively great fat posteriors.

TIME FOR CLOCK TALK
(AT THE SHOP OF MR CROCKET, WATCHMAKER)

The watchmaker was famed and skilful
At keeping clocks going, and his till full.
A man of baldness and benevolence,
No hair upon his pate showed prevalence.
You'd say, "Good morning, Mr Crocket!"
Produce your watch from wrist or pocket,

Upon which he would cast a frown,
Forewarn he'd charge you half-a-crown,
Advise, "Come back again next week
By which time it will go tick-teek."
One talked till just the hour, - which mattered,
For at that time the whole place clattered

As every clock which was available,
Displayed upon his shelves as saleable,
Or hung precariously on hooks
In every cranny, in all nooks,
Some made of copper, some of brass,
Some 'neath the counter made of glass,

Or stood within a corner solemn
Grandfather mounted on a column
Enclosing, he'd depend upon,
A single swinging pendulum
Which hung and swung ar-tick-ulate
To tell the time most accurate,

Whichever corner you might browse in
You'd count that stock of clocks a thousand,
For countless types he kept in stock,
Incredible that sound 'tick-tock'!
But STOP, and WATCH! The hour has beckoned!
Due to arrive in one split-second!

As each some mechanism releases
An orchestra of countless pieces
Must interrupt all trite discussion
Reproving it with stern percussion;
All ticks and tocks give way to chiming
Together, yet with varied timing,

Some clanging bells, or beating gongs,
Some sounding like Big-Ben's ding-dongs;
There even is a wee bird who
Will say, "Cuckoo, cuckoo" to you.
Ah! - What experience unique!
Yet all is in the past, - antique!

We heap upon our clocks no flattteries
As now they're only run by batteries!
For in this age of obsolescence
They give less pleasure by their presence.
For watchmakers, the time's run out;
Less hec-tick is their time, no doubt!

PART 4

A FEW FOOD-FOUNDED REMARKS,
COMPLIMENTS TO A COMPETENT CHEF,
TASTES IN FOOD AND TASTE FOR SPORT.

A DELICIOUS DISH
FOR BREAKFAST
(ALSO SUITABLE FOR SUPPER)

A dish the French call PIEMONTAISE
One may prepare with greatest ease.
Immersed in sauce of mayonnaise, -

One mixes de-shelled hard-boiled oeufs
With what augments those eggs enough
To make worth-while the served-up stuff.

Add colour, and enhance its flavour,
With chopped tomatoes, plus the savour
Of cooked potatoes, salt and pepper,

Then cut-up-small by sharpened knives
Some garlic, - which prolongs our lives -
Together with some chopped-up chives.

Then serve it cold, - you must not heat it, -
In servings large as they are needed
By those who simply sit and eat it, -

While finding that your ready dish is
Both palatable and delicious.
Stir into it your fondest wishes!

BAGLESS HAGGIS

If what you lack's a haggis-bag,
No need to get into a flummox,
For nowadays a plastic bag
Can serve instead of those sheeps' stomachs

Obtaining which of course entails
From inside that de-gutted sheep
A separation from entrails
Then laying aside its muttoned meat.

No tummy-bag I found available,
And so I asked the local butcher
If he would order one as saleable,
But what arrived just held no future.

By gad! I gave a gasp, - a loud 'un!
So misinformed he'd been, - mistaken,
Its pong so strong it smelt of cow-dung,
Disgustingly deformed, mis-shapen!

The idea wouldn't really win;
Instead I'd take the trouble perhaps
To bung it in the wheelie-bin,
Then cook the meat in bubble-wraps.   (but didn't).

Though HAGGIS, as was first invented,
Was always bagged by old tradition,
Without a bag being now presented
My haggis-meat came to fruition.

The moral is, for haggis-bags,
If tummy-bags from sheep one lacks,
One has to grab what bags one has
Or just make do with plastic sacks.

SYDNEY COUPE'S SUPER COOKING

(PREFERABLY SUNG TO THE MELODY OF "SONG OF THE CLYDE")

Let us sing a song which may not last too long

About the famous food that Syd pro-duces

Let it lin-ger long in our di-ges - ti-on

That we may sa-vour all its tas-ty jui-ces,

For so good is Syd at ser-ving su-per food

That no one e-ver hears a word com-plain-ing,

For of Syd-ney Coupe no-body e-ver could

While the King of Food's supreme-ly reigning.

[NOTE: It goes without saying, that these "Compliments to the Chef" verses may be adapted according to the PERSON PROVIDING and the menu provided. Should the toast-master happen to be a non-singer, he may deliver the discourse by the spoken word. Q.V.]

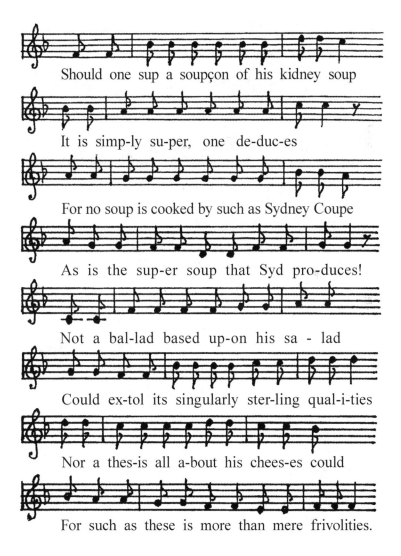

Should one sup a soupçon of his kidney soup

It is simp-ly su-per, one de-duc-es

For no soup is cooked by such as Sydney Coupe

As is the sup-er soup that Syd pro-duces!

Not a bal-lad based up-on his sa - lad

Could ex-tol its singularly ster-ling qual-i-ties

Nor a thes-is all a-bout his chees-es could

For such as these is more than mere frivolities.

REFRAIN:

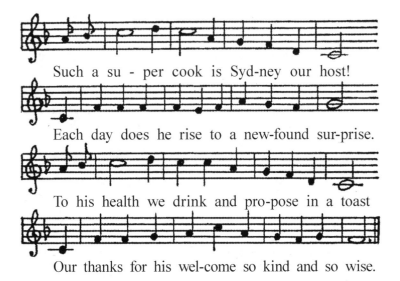

Such a su - per cook is Syd-ney our host!

Each day does he rise to a new-found sur-prise.

To his health we drink and pro-pose in a toast

Our thanks for his wel-come so kind and so wise.

2. Being a person never parsimonious,
    He in-variab-ly is so unselfish,
   As with patient care prepares for those of us
    Who enjoy a dish of tasty shell-fish
   Be they crabs or lobsters, maybe langoustines
    Or possibly a plate of prawns prepared
   Shrimp-ly marvell-ous if served with aubergines
    For never effort had he ever spared.

   Highly astronomic his things gastronomic
    That we want to eat the plate as well,
   Every trifle more than just an eyeful
    And his jellies suit the belly very well.
   Of the cakes that he so very ably bakes,
    Marzipaned and iced, fruit-filled with cherry,
   For each plateful laid before us table-mates
    We feel so grateful for it makes us merry!

                                          (REF.)

A LITTLE LIGHT
LYRIC on LENTILS

I'd been across to visit Gerard, -
A friend I'd long since kent, -
From Belgium on an urgent errand
To where he lived in Kent.

A gentleman was Gerard, true;
He heard my loud lament
That LENTILS orange-red in hue
Were hard to find in Ghent,

Though lentils there were plentiful
In yellow, green, or black,
Were red ones scarce available, -
A lamentable lack!

And so upon my journey back
Aboard that North-Sea boat,
He'd left me such a generous pack
To carry back afloat.

The Crew, concerned about its weight,
I feared would fair be frightened,
So just left undeclared my freight
To leave them unenlightened.

By methods underhand I managed
To smuggle all aboard,
The packaging left quite undamaged
Below my berth being stored.

But Gerard's eyes were slightly misting
　　As I departed seawards;
He said he'd seen the vessel listing
　　Decidedly to leewards,

Quite sure the vessel was inclined
　　Unto the left to lean,
Or "Port" in language more inclined
　　To suit the sea-ward scene.

Was it those lentils left it listing
　　Or just my heavy conscience?
Ah! - soon my slumber was insisting
　　Such sentiments were nonsense!

My sack of cargo boxed in cardboard
　　That journey would survive;
Those lentils leaning now to larboard
　　In port would safe arrive.

Now, would the Customs perhaps be puzzled
　　At such odd contraband
Below their very noses smuggled
　　Back to that foreign land?

No need had I to fear the worst
　　About such precious cargo
Les Douanes, doing their duty first,
　　Assured, "There's no embargo."

I wrote to thank that gentleman
　　On getting to Ostend . . .
"God bless you, Gerry, Lentil-man!
　　My admirable friend."

TALKING OF TASTES
"DE GUSTIBUS NON EST DISPUTANDUM"
OF GANDERS AND OF GEESE AT RANDOM.

Disputing on the taste of wine
Must surely be a waste of time,
    As some prefer it white or red
    Or rosé-pink perhaps instead.

Like humour, some enjoy it dry
According to the food they try,
    While others like to taste it sweet
    To help wash down the food they eat.

The French say, "Chacun a son goût" -
"What may suit me may not suit you",
    But should the chevron be left out,
    It seems they suffer from the gout!

"De goostibus" the Romans said
Meant not that their dear goose was dead,
    And neither "non est disputandum"
    Meant, "Let us slay the goose at random".

For in those days we now call "olden"
The goose did they esteem as golden,
    Held ever since in high regard,
    For geese in gaggles mounted guard . . .

Much more than merely muddy waders,
They'd warded-off warlike invaders,
    Who tried to capture ancient Rome,
    And still those geese goose-stepping roam . . .

Not only round about the farm,
But where there's need to sound alarm
   By means of rather raucous squeaks
   Emerging from their bills, or beaks.

That ever-fertile feathered fowl,
Flesh never flawed by flavours foul,
   Though legs and beak are quite inedible,
   Lays eggs of such a size incredible!

With nothing being consigned to waste,
Her meat yields multi-varied taste
   In regions lean or areas fatty,
   From which we make foie-gras or paté.

Before the days of "Bics" and "Biros"
The goose obligingly supplied us
   With quills designed for scrawling scrolls
   As pens perform their writing-rôles.

Her feathers made those quills, equipping
One's writing-desk with pens for dipping
   Into one's bottle of SWAN ink,   (Brands of ink at one
   Alternatively ink called QUINK.   time well-known)

We well may ask what use is in
Developing a goosy-skin?
   Forewarns us on the very second
   We may be feeling faintly threatened.

A goose induced to reproduce
First needs a husband to seduce,
   In fact, - we talk no propaganda -
   She really needs a proper gander!

CONCERNING THE SELECT SANDWICH-SHOP

A shop new and swish was set-up in Lancashire
To serve every wish in affairs of their sandwich-hire,
Or, should one say, sandwiches offered for sale
As no one was likely to bring them back stale.

They'd cut them to shape as their clients decided,
Yet always would make their triangles three-sided
Invariably varying their fare, for fair-deal
Implied they should fairly supply a square meal.

"A sandwich of salad? Going off on your honeymoon?
She'd certainly lay-on a spread from her honey-spoon.
"No, all that we need is just lettuce alone,
Then all that we plead is just let us alone."

The lady who lays on the filling's an expert on
Whatever should please your internal digestion,
Quite Krafty on cheeses, on these she'd excel,
As expert with eggs that she served minus shell.

Variety vast, when times opportune are
For sardines de-tinned, or salmon or tuna,
Tomatoes, chopped chives, or gammon thin-sliced,
Spread lightly with mustard, then peppered or spiced.

Of course of her customers some were such funny ones
By preference prompted to pick pickled onions,
Whilst others whose tastes just seemed slightly the posher
Would awkwardly ask if the nosh were quite kosher!

And so, whatever the filling or spread,
Its Lancashire patrons were always well-fed,
For even encumbered with cheese and cucumbers
That output of sandwiches doubled in numbers.

The shop that they started in Bury quite singly,
Grew branches that burgeoned as far-off as Bingley,
Then Bradford and Burnley plus Bolton and Blackburn,
Till business in Blackpool eventually tagged on.

A word of advice she'd impart to her shoppers:
"Please note our aversion to those litter-droppers,
Refusing the fact we prefer folks respectable
Accepting for wrappers the refuse-receptacle."

THE KNIFE
SOME COMMENDATORY IF CUTTING COMMENTS

Of mankind's tools in their utility
What others boast such versatility?
What instrument of all utensils
Can cut up meat or sharpen pencils,
De-gut a rabbit, trout, or sturgeon,
Equip a joiner, scout, or surgeon?

Can whittle, shave, or shape some wedge
Submitting to its keenest edge,
Create some object carved from wood,
Or else assists preparing food,
Tomatoes, onions, or cucumber,
Thin-sliced too many times to number?

No knife feels menaced by some rival,
Nor threat against its self-survival,
For other tools, it seems apparent,
Regard the KNIFE as being their parent.
Consider well the following facts
About the chisel, saw, or axe:

A CHISEL's but a knife designed
To gouge out channels well-defined;
A SAW is but a' knife serrated,
Whereas the adroit AXE is weighted
To cut through tree-trunks, logs, or heads, -
Calls executioners from their beds!

Midst other cutters miscellaneous,
The humble SPADE cuts soil terraneous,
May hollow out some earthly groove
For bodies which no longer move
Subjected to death's GUILLOTINE,
Then throws down earth to fill it in.

A surgeon skilled in sure-precision
Requires a SCALPEL for incision,
Excising with much care intensive
Some growth which could become immense if
Subjected not to his sharp knife which
Is utilised to save some life with!

While only damage sadly sordid
Is wrought by weapons, as the SWORD did,
By slicing through some some soldier sorrier
Condemned to die, - poor hapless warrior!
Oh! when will men realise that swords
Brought only death as their rewards?

Your POCKET-KNIFE if kept well-whetted
Will serve you well, - you'll not regret it.
Remove all rust, keep polished, oil it,
For loving care can never spoil it.
A blunt knife serves no purpose other.
Than opening letters, spreading butter!

SPORT AND NON-SPORT
COGNIZANT OF THE FACT THAT SPORT, LIKE EVERYTHING ELSE,
MUST SURELY HAVE ITS GOOD SIDE AND ITS BAD SIDE.

GOLF: GOOD AND BAD

Good golfers round a course cavort,
To drive a ball afar for sport.
They traipse to where the ball has gone
From where it had been driven from,
Then, putt-ing first things first, of course,
Repeat the process round the course.

While some who most need exercise
Contribute to their over-size
By planking upon caddy-cars
Their ever-fattening flabby arse,
Oh! what a travesty of sport that be
To take an armchair after tee!

FOOTBALL: GOOD AND BAD

While FOOTBALL, . . hardy, healthy sport,
Releases energy, - a different sort -
Wherein fast feet pursue the ball
Propelling it towards its goal.
By spirit, healthy competition
Quite contrary to sad division . . .

Fomented by those few fanatics
With venom in their upper attics
Who seek to spoil the sportive season.
Called "FOUL" by referees with reason! . . .
Assigning to each side a fair chance
While tolerating no intolerance.

TENNIS: GOOD AND BAD

(A NONDESCRIPT DESCRIPTION MOST CERTAINLY
NEVER VERSIFIED BY ALFRED, LORD TENNYSON)

As often said, and often written
Lawn tennis came from France to Britain,
Great Britain, - at one time being known as,
While colonising, sought the bonus
Of nations far, wherefrom the infections
Of tennis spread in all directions,

The ball going back and forth attack-ed
By players twain, each armed with racket,
While audiences vast numerically
Cheer players on hysterically,
While sport, some say, should be done _by_ us
And not just _for_ us. - Be this bias?

CRICKET: INDIFFERENT

The English have a strange religion
Which needs no rigid definition,
But name-wise seems to rhyme with wicket.
Where wickets stand, the Batsmen stick at,
While Bowlers try to strike the middle one
With no ball bigger than a little one.

Each player, clad in white regalia,
From India, Pakistan, Australia,
Wears knee-pads white, white shirt, white jumper,
Traditional to the British Umpire.
Whatever awful view one has thereon,
An Oval view may one set eyes upon.

GAME OF CHESS
THE UPS AND DOWNS OF FIERCE COMPETITION, AND CASES WHERE
IT SIMPLY ISN'T CRICKET!

A game that's usually played indoors
May yet, outside on chequered floors,
Be played by players with poles provided
Once 'black' or 'white' by vote's decided.

The game may last for minutes, hours,
Or days, - depending on the powers
Possessed by foresight intellectual
Which plans those plots and moves effectual.

On every board of chess are pieces,
Of differing heights and separate species
First, eight small soldiers, each a PAWN,
Must wait on squares they're placed upon

Until commanded to do battle,
Then must take on the task they tackle,
In one or other royal defence
Paraded with much loyal pretence,

Their captain being a KING of some sort.
Perhaps he's just the QUEEN's dumb consort,
For SHE it is who rules the roost
To whom all subjects must adjust.

A BISHOP with a mitred visor,
On each side stands as royal advisor,
His moves are more than merely marginal
As moves he back and forth diagonal.

'Twas never said that 'Good' Queen Bess
Was ever very good at Chess,   (Elizabeth 1
She'd take a KNIGHT out now and then,   1558-1603)
Then have a good night out with him!

A checkered life indeed she had
By many held less good than bad;
How could a Queen so callous be
Unless consumed by jealousy?

There is a CASTLE in each corner.
If one should hold a Queen, please warn her,
Should she be Scots and known as Mary
Of cousin Bess should she be wary.

For castles were congenial never
To Mary, who'd escaped however
From one upon Loch Leven's Isle
Imprisoned there a year-long while.   (1567-1568)

She fled to England where her cousin
Was overcome with jealous passion,
For Mary, most attractive truly,
Was jailed by cousin Liz, then duly,   (1568)

Just after nineteen years a prisoner,   (Fotheringhay)
Queen Bess decided to get rid of her.
Unto the chopping-block being led,
Dear Mary sadly lost the head!   (1587)

We face the ever-tragic moral,
Should Queens face Queens locked-up in quarrel,
That castles draughty be not scenes
For keeping, - check, mate! - rival Queens!

PART 5

ACCIDENTS, HOSPITAL OPERATIONS,
LETTERS OF SYMPATHY, LETTERS OF
THANKS.

WHY WRITE LETTERS?
'WHAT ONE WRITES WITHOUT EFFORT
RISKS BEING READ WITHOUT PLEASURE'

Here followeth the letter-press
    Upon procedures some regard less
Than others who prefer to press
    On blissfully regardless.

Should writing letters seem a nuisance,
    Some yet give pleasure once they're read.
Receiving such can give one new sense
    Of being alive instead of dead.

Much more perhaps in half the space
    May one express, if said succinctly.
Your correspondent need not chase
    Its message if it's said distinctly.

Amongst an hundred sent to friends
    In high hopes they be quite amused,
Should chance occur that one offends,
    Attempt some tact to be excused.

Of course, conditions may be various,
    To which one must adapt, according
To circumstances, sometimes serious
    In which case, get the appropriate word in.

A few examples follow typical
    Addressed to folk in hospital,
By no means merely mythical,
    To memory not lost at all.

HOSPITAL MAIL
ADDRESSED TO A PROFESSIONAL PAINTER PATIENT

A letter just to take your mind off
    Your recent visit to the theatre.
Dramatic? Sure! But not the kind of
    Performance most folks feel no fear for!

And yet, we've made the great discovery
    Of good news coming from Ward-Six.
It seems you've made a great recovery
    Since having lost your app-en-DIX!

No loss! Your cast-iron constitution
    Sufficed to show such stern resistance,
Assisted by your resolution
    To keep submission at a distance.

It be your paint-pot pals feel fainter
    Without your self to swell their ranks
With one less brush and one less painter
    To tread those trestles tied to planks.

Your motor-cycling pals still meet
    Around the local village-square
Their engines revving, soon to greet
    Your *patient* self, once more back there.

Do as you're told now, in the Ward!
    A foolish fellow's fate the worse is,
With no sure cure, and no reward
    For disobeying those nice young nurses.

Their shapely figures keep admiring
    While under care of their domain,
As we shall meanwhile be enquiring
    About the date you're back again.

BAT BITE!

A DISTANT RELATIVE REPORTED FROM BOTSWANA THAT, WHILE
ATTEMPTING TO FONDLE A BAT, THE UNAPPRECIATIVE CREATURE
IMPARTED A BITTER BITE. THE COUNTRY HAS SINCE BEEN RE-
NAMED BATSWANA.

My fine and far-off friend, dear Pat,

Your latest saddest news is that
You have been bitten by a bat!
Or otherwise could it be written:
By bat have you been badly bitten!

What motives had persuaded it
To such extremes as having bit?
You surely should have shouted "Sshugar!
Now sshift, you sshtupid little booger!"

Quite possibly it could not see
That utter criminalitee
Which drove it to dig in its claws
To grab the victim of its jaws!

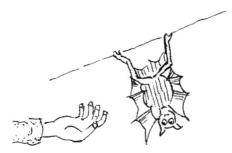

Long time no doubt it hung around
As bats will do, before it found
At last an unsuspecting victim
So tasty that its lips it licked 'em!

While so enjoying your blood for dinner
Lapped up in that late evening's glimmer,
It sought to sample while it could
That pleasant change, - your British blood!

But countered by an apt injection
Thus saved by medical protection,
Have you survived, the tale to tell
About that bat who'll burn in hell

For that dire deed, no more to fly,
But justice done, condemned to die.
Your human blood he'd sucked, so, Pat,
That hapless bat just said, "That's that!"

UNFORTUNATE FALL

(LETTER OF CONDOLENCE ADDRESSED TO AN ELDERLY LADY
WHO HAD TRIPPED AND FALLEN ON A FAULTY PAVEMENT IN PORT-
GLASGOW, FRACTURING HER HIP)

Dear Anna Petrie,

You hardly will remember that
    In times now long since past
You met the chap who's tapping out
    This letter at long last.

He's known by name as Maxwell, -
    Sad he wasn't called Dimitri,
As then he'd have the honour
    Of a name to rhyme with Petrie!

Along the bonnie coast of Clyde,
    It seems your great achievement
Was making maximum impression
    Upon the local pavement!

One hears you cracked it open wide,
    It not being *your* fault solely,
For nobody had warned you that
    You'd walk on ground so holey!

The local press reported
    That a great resounding crack
Re-echoed all the way as far
    As Gourock, there and back!

But no one knew for certain
    As they heard it in amazement
If the din came from your hip
    Or from the split upon the pavement!

We know the task is difficult
    For hard-worked HIP-noticians
Who make replacement bits for
    Broken bones in cracked conditions.

So, Anna, please henceforth refrain
    From causing further damage
To pavements of Port-Glasgow, -
    But preserve them, plus your image!

Remember how you marched so smartly
    When in the war-time A.T.S.   (Auxiliary
In khaki uniform attired,   Territorial
    And topped by khaki hats?   Service)

Well, that's how you must march again
    Along the esplanade,
But first we'll get the pavement patched,
    Once your account is paid.

And as your daily view looks out
    Upon that panorama,
We pray you'll duly feel relief
    From that most tragic trauma,

For, given gentle loving care
    And daily lubrication,
Your pains are sure to disappear,
    Replaced by jubilation!

    Happy recovery!

"IS THAT THE WEY YE AYEWAYS GET AFF THE CAUR?"

NON-FATAL FALL FROM TRAM

"PASSENGERS MUST NOT ENTER OR LEAVE THE TRAM WHILE IN
MOTION" - NOTICE IGNORED BY A NOTORIOUS SURVIVOR.

Those trams of old had platforms draughty
    On which - at stops - one stepped,
At jumping off between at speed - lads crafty
    Were dangerously adept!

Alarming the conductress so,
    Her nerves all set on edge,
This lad jumped off, but stumbled so
    And landed on a sledge!

A sledge which just then served as such
    He'd carried in his hand,
Unknowing he'd depend so much
    On that suitcase to land!

The suitcase proved a blessing, for
    It slid on harmlessly!
Surprising scene for passengers
    Within the tram to see!

As on the sleigh-ride slid quite harmless,
    So changed the driver's face
He stopped, then carried on regardless
    Saying, - "Most unusual case!"

Conductresses had always wry ways
    Expressing their vernacular:
"Is that the wey, young man, ye ayeways
    Get aff the caur? - Spectacular!"

CYCLE-LOGICAL CONSOLATION

TO GRANDSON FALLEN OFF BIKE, - WITH
ADVICE TO GUARD AGAINST RECURRENCE

My phone rang on Monday,
The day after Sunday,
And guess who it was?
Your Mother, because
She felt that she had to say
About your catastrophe.

Your crash was a bad yin
Which I must imagine
Was one dreadful skid
You skilfully did,
The ground being discovered
To be with blood covered!

Such apalling disgrace
Had befallen your face!
Inflicted such injuries
You had to have stitches
Sewn up in the surgery, -
An urgent emergency!

It can't have been pleasant
Yet won't be incessant
Because Mother-Nature
Is certain to make sure
From this awful set-back
To normal you'll get back.

You'll feel for a wee bit
A wee-bitty wabbit,
So just take things easy,
And though it won't please thee,
Allow a brief rest
To your bike. Do your best . . .

To realise in future
The road may not suit your
Attempts on such tough-stuff
So ride on less rough-stuff!
Wherever you travel
Ride never on gravel!

For gravel is treacherous;
Can upset the best of us,
And some sudden bend
Can cause blood on sand.
Just once this auld devil
Got scraped by much gravel,

Though not on his head,
But his elbow instead.
I say without kidding
The worst cause for skidding
Is turning sharp corners,
As sharp elbows warn us!

OUR DEBT TO OUR DOCTOR

OUR HEAVENLY BODIES, - yes heavenly bodies!
We have ours on hire, as has everybody,
For no one can ever the evidence find
By plans of mankind were they ever designed.

For every activity sure do we need them,
Our physical duties ensure that we feed them
Which fact, on the face of it, appears elementary
As food passes down our canal alimentary

Reposing a while in the bag that retains
Its content of nourishment feeding our veins
Until what's not wanted, once well past our waist,
Must just be ejected, and passed out as waste.

So why of our God-given gifts be ashamed?
For even our motor-cars function the same,
Until they get worn-out, their cause now a lost one,
Get flung on the scrap-heap, now dead from exhaustion.

Our skeletal frame, that bag of old bones
Strange system of plumbing each one of us owns!
No matter how skinny I seem, or how fat am I,
I'm sure Doctor John can mend my anatomy.

And yet, as we face our eventual decay,
Our spirits still strive after that brighter day.
While no other creatures on earth even think of it,
Us beings unique feel just the instinct for it.

Yet, dear Doctor John, we may have to face
The prospect of meeting in quite the wrong place,
Be sober be vigilant, the devil our adversary
May just be preparing the place that is necessary!

DOCTOR'S QUESTION-TIME

US SPIRITUAL BEINGS ARE SO LINKED-UP WITH OUR PHYSICAL
BODIES, THAT WE MUST TAKE THE LATTER ALONG TO OUR
DOCTOR NOW AND THEN. BUT SPARE HIM FROM UNNECESSARY
CONSULTATIONS, AS YOUR OWN SPIRITUAL RESOURCES CAN WORK
WONDERS.

"My Doctor-friend, dear Doctor John,
    You kent I'd been post-operational;
How kind of you to show concern
    In terms so conversational."

"My health could I not talk about
    Had I emerged less live than dead."
"Just how's it hanging?" - "Hangs no doubt,
    But only by your surgeon's thread."

"How are those legs you're standing on?"
    "The only ones I've ever had! -
They're hardly worth the handing on
    To my dear daughter and my lad."

"Yet shall I try whatever means
    To benefit them by degrees,
As they'd inherited my genes
    They too may claim my dungarees."

"Those legs are still a standing joke
    Until some stroke of luck proves fatal.
Then may you probe, as doctors poke,
    Pronouncing life's no longer vital."

"Your breathing keeps on respirating?
    Still let your lungs continuous give
That breath of life so death-defeating,
    Till no more have they lung to live?"

"I see the problem with your heart:--
    It still refuses to stop beating!"
Admitting his profession's art
    Must never slyly stoop to cheating.

"We should ensure its efforts heartily
    To tick are taken not in vain
They pump one's blood through every artery,
    Then back by air-conditioned vein."

"How are your kidneys? - still unsevered?
    Loose-liver that you've always been!
From fates far worse you've been delivered,
    Yet still possess your store of spleen."

"No, it's my nerves get up folks' noses,
    Without intention, cause offendings."
"They'll die, those nerves, states my prognosis,
    For nerves are all supplied with endings."

"They see me sometimes irritated;
    My temper gets cantankerous
Yet so far this has not created
    Great problems for my pancreas."

"Your bowels, how go they in their movements?"
    "All over Europe," came my answer;
"In Prague they Czeched them for improvements
    Through Holland, Germany, and France, sir."

"While at the bottom of the matter,
    It functions still by fits and starts,
Through many years grown rather fatter,
    Still comfortably sits and farts?"

"To change the topic, how's your brain?
    Your cavern intellectual?"
"Just now and then my cranial pain
    Tells me how ineffectual."

"Your forehead has forfeited much
    Of that to which you'd fallen heir,
A little baldly features such
    In patches there of fallen hair."

"I'm glad you've overcome your back-aches!
    No more your pained expostulations!
We're better off with backs that lack aches.
    Improve your postural positions!"

"Now should our puritanic nation
    Decree that your innate reaction
Forbids all talk on urination,
    View such as purely piddling action".

"What happened to my last prescription
    To shrink your sadly swelling prostate?"
"It would have worked, had it the option,
    But, as it turns out, I have lost it!"

At drinking problems when described
    Dear Doctor hardly laughed at all,
But golden whisky he prescribed
    To cure my lack of alcohol!

HOSPITAL HOSPITALITY

A BRIEF LETTER OF THANKS TO HOSPITAL STAFF
FROM A GRATEFUL PATIENT

I woke up in hospital to find
My small operation all behind . . .
No, not in time, but rather upon it.
By plenty of 'scope', a little light on it,
The surgeon could see on peering along
The length of a tube where sun never shone.

Although fine physicians can't make us immortal,
I'd not have emerged through your hospital portal
Had you and your team not proved so professional.
I'd surely have ceased along life's processional
Had not distinguished surgeon Stanley
Precisely and accurate acted so calmly.

By his anaesthetist well guided,
With concentration undivided,
He'd peered within my rear-end funnel
To view the problems in that tunnel,
Had seen three boulders cause obstruction,
To leave them lying'd mean my destruction.

He'd managed not to nick the thread,
For I felt far from sick in bed,
But came to say he'd deemed it wise,
No messing: simply to excise!
Showed photos, not as you'd think
In black and white, but red and pink!

I'm also writing to record
My admiration for your Ward
Wherein, receiving me as guest,
You all performed your very best
To make me feel so much at home;
Amongst fine friends I felt I'd come.

Inadequate these clumsy verses
To sing the praises of you nurses
And recognise the well-done duties
Of those, much more than merely beauties,
So skilled inserting steel syringes
Despite their patients' whines and whinges.

You measured heart-beats, pulses, samples,
Extracting warm blood as examples,
And though your shifts with work were packed full,
You stayed so patient, kind, and tactful.
One could not find a posh hotel
To match up to your ways so well.

Observing all, - I saw some Irish,
Some English, Scots, some plump, some wirish.
Keep up your sterling work with patience,
You'll always have your grateful patients.
Midst throngs your expertise amazes,
There's always one who'll sing your praises!

Appendix: My mate, next bed, - appendicitis!
                    'Tis well we've men who mend inside us!
From him they'd wrung that woeful worm
Permitting it no more to squirm.
Though once, it's true, I lost my tonsils,
At least I've kept my twin utensils!

PART 6

ABOUT BUILDINGS, MOBILE AND STATIC.

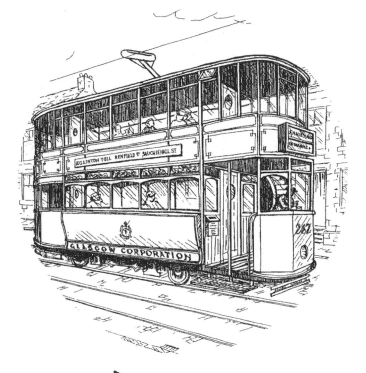

THE TRAM

"SIC TRAM SIT GLORIA MUNDI"

- TO MISQUOTE A LATIN SAYING -
"SO MAY THE TRAM BE THE WORLD'S GLORY"

The finest trams this world has known
In Glasgow's soil of course were grown
From once being single-storeyed crates
For passengers on slatted seats,
First drawn by horse-powered hooves along
Hard lines of steel with grooves thereon,

Became by power electric-cabled, -
Condemned the horse to stay en-stabled.
This power provided strength sufficient
For double-deckers driven efficient,
With passengers below enclosed,
While those up-top were left exposed

To all the elements, - yet drivers
If well wrapped-up remained survivors.
And then the bright idea was hit upon
To have the upper storey built upon.
But drivers still felt over-drafted
Till trams with outer doors were crafted.

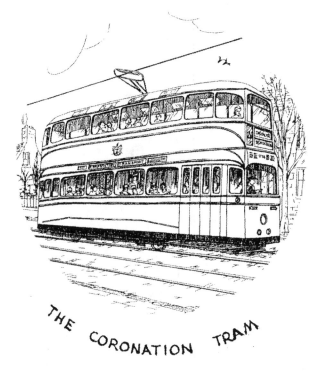

THE CORONATION TRAM

How thrilling for a lad of eight
Beholding at one tram-stop wait
A sight he never had expected!
One brand-new tram-car all electric   (1937)
Appeared, then slithered to a halt,
All quite without the usual jolt!

At once, its sleek self-closing doors
Slid open to reveal new floors
Of rubber thick, all sound-absorbing, -
No clatter from its clients boarding,
As they beheld, astonished, curious,
Plush comfort, wonderful, luxurious!

The doors slid shut. "Get aff ye cannae!"
So said the proud conductor canny   (The "conductress"
As ever present on the scene   began to assume
In uniform of bottle-green,   power as from 1939)
Collecting everybody's fares,
Then doing the same again upstairs.

Confined within his tiny cabin
The driver, shiny levers grabbing,
In silent power accelerated
Attaining speeds unprecedented.
"Let Glasgow Flourish!" some exclaimed
While its notorious slums remained!

That masterpiece of architecture
Once mobile, may, as some conjecture,
Make re-appearance to remind us
That constantly it was our kindest
Friend of friends environmentally
Which injured fewest accidentally!

SPIRES OF UNIVERSITY & CHAPEL
MEDIÆVAL REVIVAL STYLE 1868

WELLINGTON CHURCH
ROMAN-RENAISSANCE 1884

The Age of Revivalism

THE RESIDENCE of C.R. MACKINTOSH FACED BOTH THESE BUILDINGS

GLASGOW SCHOOL OF ART

1909

GLASGOW SCHOOL OF ART

Acclaimed as one of the world's first modern buildings. Designed by
Charles Rennie Mackintosh 1868-1928 and Opened 1909. A visit to the
School of Art and to the Mackintosh Museum, Hillhead Street, and to the
many Mackintosh examples is strongly recommended for those who wish
to fully comprehend the context of the concise commentary herein. An
abundance of books is available.

In Hillhead's district (rather posh)   (Southpark Avenue)
Lived Charles Rennie Mackintosh
Whose studious searchings made deduction
That all around him, reproduction
Had been the rage for many an age;
He thought it time to turn the page.
Around him while still young there grew
A spate of buildings, then quite new.

The past had duly handed down
Some Greek, some Roman. Every town
Displayed such styles historic
As Corinthian, Doric, and Ionic,
Perhaps in proud Palladian piles,
Or, for a change of ancient styles,
Some 'Mediaeval' known as 'Gothic'
Would rise again as if authentic.

He viewed by glances more than cursory
The style of Glasgow's University
Where Gilbert Scott of widespread fame
Had clad a basic cast-iron frame
Perpetually and proudly posed
In 'Early English' fancy clothes.
'Of one thing quite convinced I am:
That face of stone is such a sham!'

ENTRANCE FAÇADE : SCHOOL of ART

While Alex Thomson from Balfron
Imposed his Classic style upon
The face of Glasgow's fine façades -
His Grecian touch still masquerades,
Occasionally showing addiction
To ornamental forms Egyptian.
Most clever, his creations speak
Of Glasgow having gone quite Greek!

Said Mackintosh, 'Let's stop all this! -
No future for the Acropolis!
It's time we thought in terms contemporary.'
Yet Scottish styles from some past century
Combined with features formed from nature
He fused into new architecture
Of human style and scale, not brutal
Like some which since have turned out futile

Viz: certain continental 'masters'
Whose modern efforts, now disasters
Of crumbling concrete caged in crates
Have earned at last their fallen fates!
When boxes brashly boast being hailed
As 'architecture' then they've failed!
But attitudes of harsh austerity
Lost Charles to Scotland for posterity.

From much indifference he suffered
Dismayed, he just retired to Suffolk.
But meanwhile let us view his own work
Designed in timber, glass, and stonework,
Displaying itself to those who're able
To cast an eye upon that gable
Which many have in film encaptured
By its fantastic form enraptured.

THE ART SCHOOL LIBRARY

The challenge of those slopes of Scott Street
Was one most people thought he'd not meet, -
And yet with measured skill he'd rise
To asymmetrical surprise! . . .
Those small-squared windows rising upwards
All set in shafts of stone smooth-surfaced
Alongside coursed and textured rubble
Against which glass forms contrast double, -

All not without those humorous touches
Included in his concepts, such as
That corner-studio he endeavoured
To jut out quaintly cantilevered!
Such shapes fail not to fascinate
Some seen upon no previous date,
But based on Nature's inspirations
In wood detailed, or wrought-iron railings.

To uniformity indifferent,
Each wall appearing wholly different,
He worked out every elevation
As being a separate revelation.
Though stunning is the main north front,
His most outstanding daring stunt
Lies in that library of storeys twain,
Where bookshelves hang in galleries fine

Lit up by lamps hung high as pendants.
What bookworm can resist ascendance
Towards such heights of inspiration
As radiate from that creation
Whose light and shade alternate-wise
Delight the aspiring artist's eyes?
Light lying between each airy space
Where shadows haunt the enlightened place!

CHARTRES CATHEDRAL

CATHEDRAL-CRAWLING

To souls sadly sensing directionless drifting
Cathedrals supply much essential uplifting,
For though their construction be solid materially,
They speak, so it seems, to their throngs quite ethereally.

To many folk Chartres still a favourite remains;
Once passed through its portals, such spiritual gains
Are gradually gathered from atmosphere mellowed
By rich light through stained-glass for centuries hallowed.

The human race still seeks those shrines of sublimity,
Each one of them storing some spark of divinity
Which lights up that flame seeking solace beyond us
In states of much promised and sought-after wonders.

Mere men made Cathedrals, but men who were fired
By spiritual uplift which stirred and inspired
Their craft's ceativity, freely expressed
Through tools of their trades and love of what's best.

In Britain that craftsmanship truly was comparable
With styles shipped from Normandy, England being conquerable.
One feels the full strength of each solid stone column
In Durham Cathedral, or Scotland's Dunfermline.

The pointed style, Gothic as often mis-called,
Changed arches and churches to structures thin-walled,
Till gradually houses of glass, - don't throw stones!
Emerged in which bishops could safely stow thrones.

That style spread through England and Scotland, even Orkney,
With vibrant vitality, never monotony,
Gave elegant poise shaping stones from our mountains
Into Abbeys like Rivaulx, Crossraguel, and Fountains,

ARCHITECTURAL EXCEPTIONS

THE PETERBOROUGH PUZZLE

That portico's array of arches
    Still pose perpetual riddle
As why they hadn't placed the largest
    Directly in the middle

ONE WONDERS IN WELLS

In Wells Cathedral, 'neath the tower,
    Thus structurally braced
Supporting arches numbering four
    Have upside-down been placed.

LIVERPOOL CATHEDRAL
(N° 2: The "Mersey Funnel")

In recent times a new conception
    Of outworn styles non-typical
Has changed to popular perception
    The old skyline of Liverpool.

Set Tintern and Bolton in scenic surrounding,
Lincluden and Sweetheart midst others abounding,
Like Melrose and Jedburgh, Holyrood, Kelso.
Yet all those lay ruined! Iona was also.

To rubble reduced, destroyed by deformers,
As many regard those misguided 'reformers',
Who bear by the fruits of their wide-ranging ravages
A shameful repute as but wild raging savages

As if those vile vandals were not more than bad enough
Destroying Saint Andrew's, still worse that man Badenoch
Who razed the Cathedral of Elgin so elegant
To such a sad state well-past re-development.

Our culture was cut down by fearsome strikes frightening;
York Minster seemed lightly let off, struck by lightning!
But though such destruction was direly deplorable,
Yet Paisley, Iona, Dunblane, proved restorable.

By contrast, when times were more kind than political,
The skills of our craftsmen proved crucially critical,
For buildings became stone-framed houses of glass
Attaining such standards as none could surpass.

To quote William Wordsworth, such buildings immense
Are long since revered as being worth the expense
Like King's College, Cambridge, or Henry-seventh's Chapel
Whose out-branched fan-vaulting still spreads without topple.

Instead of staying static to loaf around lazily,
See each one in turn, from the Abbey at Paisley
To Glasgow, then Edinburgh, head southwards to Manchester,
Newcastle then Durham, leave Lichfield for Winchester.

For even a Scotsman brought up on thick porridge
Should cherish the chance to see Chester and Norwich,
And sort out his circuit so terribly cleverly
That none be left out, such as Selby or Beverley.

Gothic Constructional Principles

Do visit the Minster of York! Also nip in
North-west a few miles to the Cathedral of Ripon.
Not far to the south while you've still legs to limp on
The 'Imp' will extend you warm welcome at Lincoln.

View Ely's fine lantern-towers rising octagonally,
See Salisbury's spire, once crossed England diagonally.
Perhaps you'll have popped in to Peterborough, thence
As pilgrim to Canterbury, - French in pretence.

Such valuable visits should voyagers well afford!
What glories at Gloucester, Bath, Worcester, Wells, Hereford!
And Westminster Abbey, beside Big Ben's chimes,
All styled in French stone after Caen's conquest-times.

Whereas its Cathedral, in brick incidentally,
Four-domed, was designed in 'Byzantine' by Bentley,
Who felt that the style which replaced 'Perpendicular'
'Renaissance' by name, was rather too secular,

Well-suited for Inigo Jones' dignified halls
Or the essence of Wren so renowned in Saint Pauls.
Some modern ones built in the twentieth century,
Are Liverpool's two, Truro, Guildford and Coventry.

If ever in Devon, endeavour no exit, or
You'd risk having missed that amazing one, Exeter!
Its many-branched vaulting all spead out like arms
Of petrified palm-trees, still singing stone psalms.

For MUSIC and ART, though not mentioned by him
Who wrote not one verse of one psalm or one hymn
Nor asked that we build any tower or high steeple,
Would yet know the needs of his Church - built of people!

Wherever one visits, wherever one starts,
It's well worth remembering to pop in to Chartres.
Once traversed the Channel, should chance grant you spare money,
First make Tour-de-France, - then head off to Germany.

BOX-LIKE BUILDINGS

THE BLAND BOX, FORMING THE FASHION OF MUCH BUILDING-
DESIGN FROM THE THIRTIES, OFTEN INVITED INGRESS OF RAIN
IN A COUNTRY WHERE FLAT-ROOF TECHNIQUES HAD NEVER
BEEN ENTIRELY MASTERED. REPLY HEREWITH TO PRESS-LETTER
BY ALEX SCOTT WHO COMPLAINED THAT, EVERY WINTER, HIS
FLAT ROOF BECAME A DAMP NUISANCE TO HIS HOUSE.

Dear Sir,

The question raised by Alex Scott
    Has hardly fallen flat
On whether roofs be pitched or not,
    For one result is that
A flood of correspondence
    In full-flood did begin;
Reactions raged in fierce abundance,
    Some 'for' and some 'agin'.

In Scotland, auld tradition reigns
    That roofs be sloped and slated
It being a land where oft it rains.
    Roofs flat are failure-fated.
And buildings box-like blend no more
    Than blots on our horizon
So ugly as aloft they sore
    Towards the skies high-rising.

One Planning Chief of this opinion,
    On seeing a flat-roofed garage,
Played all the powers in his dominion
    That eyesore to disparage.
Yet surely such a silly ass felt
    By having barked and bitched;
The builder covered it with asphalt
    Saying, "Now, you see, it's pitched!"

the
Mozarteum

BUILDINGS that BREATHE BADLY

THE MOZARTEUM, MUSIC-COLLEGE IN SALZBURG, ONCE FACED
THREAT OF CLOSURE (1998) BECAUSE OF BREATHING PROBLEMS

If Scotland has buildings by problems afflicted,
In most other nations are defects detected.
Despite, or because of, such systems "efficient"
Prescribing the modes that we breathe, air-conditioned.
We suffer infections, sore-throats, and bronchitis
From bugs that abound being hell-bent to bite us.

An Austrian College for studies in Music
Developed diseases that would have made *you* sick, -
Sick-syndrome they called it, - condition obnoxious
Pervading our present-day buildings or boxes.
By modern materials built, - tried and tested?
By up-to-date germs and by microbes infested!

Our fresh-air was once a most valued commodity,
Now shut-out from buildings all sealed-up hermetically.
Yet, - even if windows were flung-open wide,
Pollution from carbon-monoxide outside
Would enter our systems, degrading our breath,
Just slowly but surely would choke us to death!

Precinct all our cities, keep cars well away,
Hire horses and coaches, bring bikes into play.
Remember, as any researcher well kens,
That eggs are no better from battery hens
All cooped up in crates, - lack free-range defiance
Of fresh-air restrictions conditioned by Science.

BIVVY BUILT IN BAVARIA
A BUILDING THAT BREATHES FREELY

Should one wend one's way in that backwoodland area
One finds in the forests of far-off Bavaria,
You may come across a construction of canvas,
To wild winds and wet rains entirely impervious,
The canvas being stretched on a framework of pine-poles,
Arranged so that wood-smoke ascends through escape-holes,
           Fine building it is
           Fine building it be
           With no more pretence
           Than being a TEPEE,

According to him who inhabits that dwelling
For five months per year, - then back to his calling,
Called what? Do we have a Red-Indian here?
Architectural structural engineer?
Who made his own canvas-sewn masterpiece, how, boys?
By means well surpassing mere methods of Cowboys!
           In sole isolation
           Central heating had he,
           Twin-skinned insulation
           Within his TEPEE.

A stock of thick sticks had he handy to stoke up
The wood-fire he'd light every morning he woke up,
Being hooked on the food he could cook in the manner of
Old backwoodsman methods he'd long-since been master of
A stick he'd select to be used as a skewer
For sticking through mushrooms, not much room for more.
           So good to awaken,
           As fresh eggs fried he,
           To sweet smells of bacon
           From out his TEPEE.

He'd hear all those quaint calls of wild birds at play,
He'd feed little tame birds, or stray cats by day,
A bottled-gas lamp lit his vision by night
For he had disowned television outright,
Instead he would read, or would just sit and think,
Then write down on paper his thinking with ink.
        On deep thought intent,
        Philosopher he
        Content in the tent
        He called his TEPEE.

"Become independent! Discover one's worth,
Seven months in the city is more than enough!"
For provisions he'd walk to a neighbouring farmhouse,
In derision he thought all non-exercise far worse
Than exercise healthy to keep live limbs moving,
For once they are dead, they lie still, past improving.
        No need for a car
        For no car had he
        To travel not far
        From his canvas TEPEE.

Reclusive, this hermit half-hidden, half-shy,
Would welcome most warmly whoever passed by
A thin wisp of smoke from his chimney-piece rose,
Inviting a passer-by passing. . . "Who goes?
Come in", said the occupant, "No need to knock,
Just hang up your jacket, we'll chat and we'll talk
        Till midnight maybe.
        Some whisky or tea?"
        "I'll risk it", said he,
        "To praise your TEPEE!"

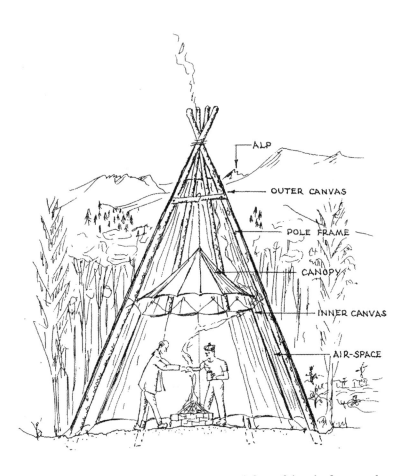

ALP

OUTER CANVAS

POLE FRAME

CANOPY

INNER CANVAS

AIR-SPACE

Thus two men, once strangers, turned firm friends for good,
Once duly downed drams went down with much food.
But, sooner or later, as nature decreed
One's natural output hath need of a spade,
Thus armed, they set out to dig their deep trench
To cover all causes of unwelcome stench.
> But should such decree
> Less serious be
> Quite simply would they
> Step outside TEPEE.

DRESDEN'S DISASTER

[AS OBSERVED 2006]

To pay condolences, long time I'd languished
To see that city agonised and anguished, . . .
For war had wrought a dreadful mess then, . .
Made sure there was but little left of Dresden.   [1945]
Ah! How one felt unutterable sadness
As one beheld destruction's utter madness!

Arriving at the re-built railway-station
One saw the signs of dreadful devastation;
Museums, churches, public-halls, - once flattened,
The Concert-Hall where opera oft-happened,
Great masterpieces architectural
All smashed to pieces by that dreadful war!

What's worse, the loss of thousands of civilians!
The human cost one cannot count in millions.
But bravely, bit by bit, and piece by piece,
They're busily re-building, since the Peace.
When will they learn, mad men of bombing nations?
They've naught to earn by such abomination!

GLASGOW BOMBARDED

1941 - ON THE PERIPHERY OF THE CLYDEBANK BLITZ

(As seen, heard, felt, regretted, and remembered)

NOTE: THE LUFTWAFFE RAIDS WERE FLOWN
FROM NAZI-CONQUERED NORWAY

Us school-boys had back from our war-time homes drifted
Fond parents imagined all threats had been lifted.
For Scotland they'd thought much too distant from strikes
As unleashed on London by Luftwaffe tykes.
But all of a sudden, in our very locality,
We found ourselves faced with the same grim reality.

The sirens would wake one with weird warning sounds
Which rose in tones terrifying, ups and then downs;
They howled as they rose, and they moaned as they tumbled,
And wailed up and down again many times numbered
Till every scared soul was awake and wrapped warm
Fleeing down to what shelter might shield them from harm.

From a glance on the way, through the window you'd realise
The light shone in shafts from searchlights on clear skies
Were scanning for bomber-planes hostile heard coming
On high from a distance with a brum-brum-brum-brumming.
They nearer and louder approached, - big guns banged,
BANG, BANG, anti-aircraft guns, more deafening BANGS!

Yet friendly, and soundly on *our* side they sounded,
For at first no dull thuds or cruel crashes resounded, -
But soon, once we'd fled to our cellar for shelter,
We heard bombs descending in wild helter-skelter
Each screeching in screams as they swiftly descended
With loud lurches landing, their dread descents ended.

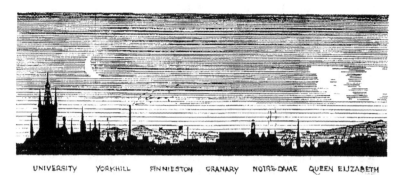

UNIVERSITY   YORKHILL   FINNIESTON   GRANARY   NOTRE-DAME   QUEEN ELIZABETH

GLASGOW in 1939 *from a house high in Hillhead*

BEFORE WAR HAD BROKEN OUT

MINE LANDING FLARES SEARCHLIGHTS BOMBS   BARRAGE-BALLOONS CLYDEBANK

GLASGOW in 1941 *from a brief glimpse*

ONCE WAR HAD BROKEN LOOSE

We knew as we stared at each other in terror
That some had just missed us, and missed us in error,
And hour after hour that raid seemed to last
Until things died down, then that sound "raiders past"
The sirens sang this time, more sweetly in tones
Which stayed up consistent in pitch, minus moans.

Our sighs of relief were sincere, and the first
Thing we turned to was tea for our thirst!
The following morning, white-faced and unslept,
We went to meet mates who from shelters had crept
To see scenes most dreadful of dire devastation
Of ruins reduced quite beyond recognition.

The B.B.C. building in Queen Margaret Drive
Was narrowly missed by a huge bomb which dived
Right into two tenements blowing them to rubble,
With Kelvin Way bearing the brunt of more trouble,
A bomb burst its bridge with an earth-shaking quiver
Huge statues of bronze being blown down to the river.

Good folk were attending to things which most mattered,
Some boarding up windows, for thousands had shattered.
In hospitals, doctors and nurses were tending
The wounded, and sewing-up their gashes for mending.
Brave firemen played hoses on buildings which burned,
And dampened-down houses to ashes now turned.

As darkness descended that evening, we saw
In Clydebank's direction an ominous red glow!
We knew what it meant, - that others were struck
Much worse than were we who'd escaped just by luck.
Our hopes that the next night might bring some repose
Proved too optimistic just to suppose.

The moon rose again with a face full and round,
Upon its next prospect unfavourably frowned,
While raiders returning regarded that moon
In aiding their aims as a blessing and boon.
Clydebank once again was their target of terror
From whence many hundreds had hurried in horror.

Same wretched routine was for several nights served
On buildings blitzkrieged and on people un-nerved
Or instantly killed for what object or reason?
Yet very much worse was to come in due season
To victims of cities turned unsafe to live in.
So senseless it seemed to a lad then eleven . . .

And others who've ever since suffered from qualms
When singing those self-righteous verses of psalms, -
"If the Lord in his might had not been on our side . ."
The other side might be unequally right?
Had Glasgow been Dresden, a town non-strategic,
We'd all have been dead then . . . from misguided logic!

The Clydebank Blitz
James Miller R.S.A.

CROSSING THE CAM BRIDGE

The bridge is called the "Bridge of Sighs"
Magnificence in micro-size,
Enhanced by snow in lines of white
Fine features all picked out to sight,
Each to the whole ensemble related
With parapet all crenellated.

Three-lighted windows poise their perch
Upon the main segmental arch
Up-rising as it spans the ice
When River Cam looks twice as nice.
We met up once upon that same bridge
Last time we both set foot in Cambridge.

PERSONAL IMPRESSIONS
OF SANTIAGO
(on a recent visit)

I'd just woken-up from a shortish siesta
Well-spent on the slats of a Spanish park-bench - ah!
Yet sheltered somewhat from the sun's scorching heat,
Palm-branches protecting that opportune seat.

But prior to leaving that pleasant green park
In order to traipse through the town before dark,
Some sweet Spanish sounds were seducing my ears
Plus people applauding with clapping and cheers.

For two youthful acrobats, - skills so enormous, -
With poise were presenting a precarious performance,
One muscular man plus a slender girl supple
Trapesing so pleasingly, bodies bent double.

Enraptured by rope-tricks, their audience feels
The hazards they chanced hanging-on by their heels!
Expressing concern once their show was quite over,
"You seem somewhat short of security-cover!

No soft mats to fall-on in case of slight slips,
Hard concrete would break your brave bodies in bits!"
"Non parlo Espagnole" I said with apology,
So signalled by sign-language, - sort-of psychology.

The man bade me speak in plain English, explaining
"My 'ome town is Manchester (!)" graciously grinning!
"My Mum joost waunt watch me; she'd seen me being born,
But seeing me being killed might joost leave 'er off-form!"

Then shortly to see the old city I crept;
At climbing its steep slopes one gets quite adept.
The train-station's steps number just fifty-four
The hostel I stayed at had forty-one more!   (95)

While copious cars cram the highways quite criminally,
From old narrow streets they're prohibited firmly;
Instead it be tourists and pilgrims who throng
The pavings with staves so to push them along.

Half-dead on arrival, departing half-live,
Had I found the old town a desirable dive.
Its streets spread like spokes from its centralised hub,
Each second shop served as a restaurant or pub.

Between which small shops sold cheap souvenirs
At prices proposed by their rich profiteers,
Some selling cheap jewellery by means of just which
The pockets of purchasers line those of the rich.

But business is never too brisk for those fellahs
Who run at the risk of not selling umbrellas,
For rain's rather rare, though a valued commodity,
With sunshine consistent being less of an oddity.

And so they stock sticks or stout staves in addition,
For walking about is the town's great tradition,
Some come from far distances, pilgrims perhaps,
So walking-sticks help to encourage such chaps!

Ignoring such shops as sold trash and cheap tat,
My ears felt attracted towards "What is that? -
It seemingly sounds like a military band
Playing music non-militant, - quite close-at-hand."

First buying from the fruit-shop two pears and two mangoes,
I paced to that place where fantastic Fandangoes,
Beguines and Boleroes, and fast Spanish Dancias
Were gracing the atmosphere. People clapped, "Gracias!'

Going on through the city's steep hills, yet not mountains,
Were places provided where children at fountains
Would splash one another with gleeful hilarity
Close-by the Cathedral, - the fount of true charity.

In style Romanesque, majestic and massive,
Despite much Baroque, it is highly impressive.
A huge CENSER high-hung is by ropes activated,
Thus dense clouds of INCENSE, when swung, are created.

Huge crowds still it serves, as those pilgrimating
Require by such ritual a full fumigating,
For pilgrims whenever together they're met,
Have a surfeit of sore-feet that smell as they sweat.

The reason those pilgrims converge on that local joint
Is due to the fact it was always a focal-point
For those who still treasure the memory of Jam-es,
Or Seamus in Irish, - thus Saint-Iago's famous . . .
        (Sp. James)
By ancient tradition, more proven than possible,
It's HE who was JAMES from the days of the Gospel,
And they buried his bones where they've ever since slept
Without which he couldn't have crept down to the crypt.

PART 7

MUSIC, COMPOSERS, A POET,
ART, ARTISTS, THE STAGE.

IN PRAISE OF A POET

ROBERT SERVICE: 1874 - 1958

Most people have heard of the poem "Dan McGrew"
But ask them perchance if the author they knew
Of that epic story become justly famous,
Or where he was born, or knew what his name is.

In Glasgow brought up, he went to that old school
Brand new in those days, and proved he was no fool.
He hated its discipline, harsh in those days,
And later left Glasgow, and city life's ways.

But first as a bank-clerk, he trained in finance,
Thus grounding him soundly, which helped him advance
To wider horizons, to hazards more dangerous
"Where glistering gold might yield up some gain for us."

So, setting out singly with rucksack and stick
In search of adventure through thin and through thick,
He found this in YUKON once traversed the ocean,
To join others hooked-on that mad GOLD-RUSH notion.

There met up with rough-guys and tough-guys and bluff-guys
Quite fed-up with wimpish or weak-guys or soft-guys.
While blazing his bold way the wild ways of Yukon through
'Amazing', he'd tell you, 'amazing what you-can do!'

'You must persevere, and put your whole mind to it,
For one never knows in some hole what you'll find in it.
You'll only discover the glory that's gold-like
Once scaled over mountains, climbed over the Klondyke.'

Now, once he'd accomplished much toil with much trouble,
He swept out an old shack with brush and with shovel,
Then furnished this chalet perched high on a hillside
With ONE cherished ally kept close to his bedside.

That friend was a hard-working typing-machine
In whom he confided the strange things he'd seen, -
Adventurous escapades, grim times and tough,
Rascals and robbers who lived and slept rough.

He tapped on that typewriter all types of tales
While never expecting the right type of sales.
Forget the old gold-rush! Those poems that he penned
Would fetch much more worth than what gold he had panned.

His readers would recognise those they had read about,
So told all their friends, and had his fame spread about.
They'd met Dan McGrew before he was shot,
Had known Sam McGhee, - to ashes burnt hot.

To quote him but briefly, 'Such strange things are done
As men moil for gold, by the midnight sun!
The Arctic trails have their secret tales
The tales that would make your blood run cold!'

Now, once he had quitted such strange-style enjoyment,
He travelled to Paris, to find full employment   (1912)
In ambulance-driving, transporting war-casualties,
Then back up to Brittany, reviving his faculties.

In writing romances nostalgic to look on
As lingered those memoirs all stored-up from Yukon,
He branched-out more widely with close observations
Of places and people - all types and conditions.

Wide-ranging in subject, wide open in mind,
Philosophy varied in poesie you'd find
Reflecting his fond admiration for Burns   (1759 - 1796)
Whose versatile verse universal praise earns . . .

As Robert Service also deserves at long last,
For no one from Hillhead School ever surpassed
His genius portraying experience so various.
Herewith one example he'd like to display to us:

THE JOY OF BEING POOR
ROBERT SERVICE (THE FIRST VERSE OF FOUR)

Let others sing of gold and gear, the joy of being rich;
But oh, the days when I was poor, a vagrant in a ditch!
When every dawn was like a gem, so radiant and rare,
And I had but a single coat, and not a single care;
When I would feast right royally on bacon, bread and beer,
And dig into a stack of hay, and doze like any peer;
When I would wash beside a brook my solitary shirt,
And though it dried upon my back, I never took a hurt;
When I went romping down the road contemptuous of care,
And slapped Adventure on the back - by Gad we were a pair;
When, though my pockets lacked a coin,
                            and though my coat was old,
The largess of the stars was mine, and all the sunset gold;
When time was made for fools, and free as air was I,
And hard I hit, and hard I lived beneath the open sky;
When all the roads were one to me, and each had its allure . .
Ye Gods! these were the happy days,
                            the days when I was poor!

AT LEIPZIG

I'd leapt into Leipzig . . . upon a pilgrimage
To see if I might seek . . . my chance for homage paid
To him from high in heaven (von Himmel hoch)   [at St Thomas
Came down to earth as John Sebastian Bach . . .   Leipzig 1723
He stepped down from his normal granite stand   to 1750]
Extending welcome by his formal outstretched hand

Then to the Kir-che bade me enter in
Where heavenly music made a wondrous din,
Not only Bach being heard in soul and spirit,
But other famed musicians sound in merit.
Composers since sincerely say their skill's
All due to him whose influence lives on still.

How Handel hailed him as a brother! . . and
How Mozart journeyed from another land,   [Austria, Vienna 1789]
Arriving not by motor-driven forces,
But carried in a coach drawn by twain horses.
The town turned out in hundreds that they might all
Hear Mozart play Bach's organ by recital . . .

Displaying such skill by amply agile fingers
In praise of Bach's non-fragile fame that lingers.
Saint Thomas' Choir sang one of Bach's Cantatas
Which so moved Mozart saying, "Such music matters!"
Another great composer, Felix Mendelssohn,
Expert on organs too with pedals on,

Essayed to rescue Bach from near obscurity
Ensuring that he'd last for all posterity,
Reviving in most reverential fashion   [1841]
Bach's masterpiece the great "Saint Matthew Passion".
Sincere felicitations Felix paid,
So later was Bach's big bronze statue made.   [1908]

Then Bonn-born Beethoven, at his piano said,
"Bach's Fugues and Preludes are my daily bread."
The famous "Forty-Eight" formed fine example;
For Shostakovicz twenty-four were ample.
Bold Brahms from Hamburg in his Symphony-Four then
Wrote ground-bassed variations, as had Bach before him.

Sure, he'd uphold those lofty works harmonic
That Leopold Stokowski plus his Philharmonic
Made orchestrations for, - and none be finer
Than Bach's Fugue-plus-Toccata in D-minor.
Then Italy's Respighi, inter alia,
Had orchestrated Bach's great Passacaglia.

Sir Edward Elgar, musically a sorcerer,
Re-wrote an organ-work for orchestra
That Bach be broadcast to a huger public . . .
A Prelude plus a rousing fugal subject.
From England also, William Walton made
A Ballet-Suite from Bach, on stage displayed . . .

"The Virgins Wise", though never played on virginals,
But by full orchestra from Bach's originals.
To classic-fans is Bach by no means limited
"Bach goes to Town" in swing-sounds uninhibited
By Bennie Goodman, proving old Bach has
A following midst certain fans of Jazz.

Strange tastes sway certain people differently,
Some turn away, hear Bach indifferently,
But Bach lives on, outliving critics all!
To learn his language well is critical.
It paid to live up to that life-long promise
And worship Bach at Kirche von Sankt Thomas.

FINGAL'S CAVE · ISLE *of* STAFFA
— WITH MENDELSSOHN & MANUSCRIPT IN FOREGROUND

FINGAL'S CAVE

ISLE OF STAFFA, SCOTLAND, ONCE
VISITED BY FELIX MENDELSSOHN

You'll find if you thumb through your ordnance map, - ah!
Just *there* is the tiny-wee island of STAFFA
    A name one might mingle
    With a giant's called FINGAL
Who found for his house a huge rock with a hole in it
And then he decided to inhabit the whole if it,

For, standing inside its commodious hollow,
He hollered to find out if echoes would follow.
    They did, "HALLOH - Halloh -
    Halloh - halloh - *halloh . . . !"*
So straightway declared that its ideal accoustic
Had he found fit to favourably class as FANTASTIC!

But Fingal vacated that cavern eventually
To make way for one who'd replace him effectually,
    Re-crossing his Causeway
    To Ireland, - a long way -
He thus left it free for a GIANT of MUSIC!
An offer so pleasing he'd hardly refuse it.

That marvellous master of music was MENDELSSOHN
Whose head had two ears, one each side, just like Handel's on.
    To Scotland being bent on
    A visit, . . he went on
A steam-boat to see those far islands called HEB-RID-ES
Since when he's remained midst Great Music's Celebrities.

Inspired by the ECHO that Fingal had yodled,
His music of STAFFA on staff-lines he juggled,
    And as he chewed o'er
    His fine Overture,
The great cave of Fingal revived visual memories
Transcribed as his Overture known as "The HEBRIDES".

MOANER ? RELEASE HER !

MONA LISA   LADY OF THE NIGHT

Upon dear Mona Lisa
    Still hanging in the Louv-re
I smiled in hopes to please her
    But simply failed to move'er.
She stared back quite unblinking
    Upon that crowd within
Without a doubt just thinking
    Mine was the sillier grin.

Amused so very slightly
    From Leonardo's brush,
She cast regard but lightly
    Without the slightest blush
Upon that gathered crowd
    Who stood around admiring,
Yet sadly unendowed
    With patience as untiring

As Mona's, who would hang
    Around till all had gone,
And then rejoicing sang
    At last being left alone.
For, out from that frame opting
    Each evening to unwind
She'd wander off, adopting
    A different frame of mind.

Her 'chanson de la nuit'
    So sweetly would resound
Avec beaucoup d'esprit
    Those galleries around
Till back into her frame
    She'd step to stay quite static,
Resuming once again
    That smile so enigmatic.

KELVINGROVE ART GALLERY

MAN IN ARMOUR

REMBRANDT: KELVINGROVE ART GALLERY

Should one come back from Paris, rove
As far as Glasgow's Kelvingrove
Wherein has hung around some time
A masterpiece of ART as fine
As that of Leonardo's "Mona"
And every bit as much a loner,

But from admiring crowds protected
By armour-plating, double-breasted,
Plus shining helmet pulled well-down
Upon his eye-brows' faintest frown,
A sword held in that grasping hand
So boldly brushed by brave Rembrandt.

Reposed, relaxed from warfare's clamour,
Still sits serene his "MAN IN ARMOUR".

MOZART

WHOSE STERNEST STATEMENTS YET STATE GLADNESS,
HIS SWEETEST SENTIMENTS SO TINGED WITH SADNESS.

The moment one mentions the music of Mozart,
Amazed at the mind that so marvellously composed it,
Some philistine *will* opine much is pure piffle,
Consider it simply a style superficial!
Of all controversial composers, this Paradox
Of orthodox styles was so often un-orthodox.

Two fellows philosophised as they meandered, -
One thought that the other chap merely philandered, -
They sat down to ease intellectual endeavour,
Graced grassy green banks of a clear rural river
Which flowed as it showed every varied occurrence
From still pools to whirlpools and turbulent currents.

Now one of them gazed on an un-ruffled surface
To duly deduce what exactly its worth is;
But all he discovered in downward direction
Was his countenance countered by mirrored reflection.
That unwilling river would nothing reveal
Apart from his face and its surface-appeal.

The other decided to dive in quite sudden
To see if the river-bed merely had mud in,
Delighted to find on reaching the bottom
New treasures lay there where they'd long lain forgotten;
All sizes of stones, some round and some slender
Resembling gems jewelled, resplendent their splendour.

PARADOXES INSCRUTIBLE

Enthralled and entranced by those treasures discovered
He realised that more could with care be uncovered!
Even oysters abounded with shells lined in gold, -
They'd fetch a fair fortune if auctioned or sold, -
So precious those pearls, their price would be doubled
By other gems gorgeous they'd grabbed and then gobbled!

But here we digress; - it's hardly too hard to see
We've roamed into realms of a far-away fantasy,
For though the analogy may easily be evident,
It risks being diverted towards the irrelevant.
Such similar similies seem all the better for
Being turned into truths told not merely by metaphor.

So back to dear MOZART whose odd contradictions
Seemed set to estrange him from human predictions,
For nothing he set out to do or endeavour
Could purely be put down to being super-clever.
He wrote at such speed, - not much time to rehearse a while,
And varied variety by being hyper-versatile.

The longest so far of his symponies we quote as
"The Linz", - for that city composed at short notice, (No. 36)
Just three days allowed him, - yet no sign of hurry,
Its slow movement spacious, relaxed, without worry!
The "Prague" followed after, then three of his last (No. 38)
Each best amongst equals, all quite unsurpassed. (39,40,41)

No instrument up to that epoch invented
He'd fail to observe, - full attention he lent it;
Some string-skimmed, or wind-blown, and even the flute,
Though first he disliked it, with ear so acute,
He none-the-less wrote for, - or else, - think how tragic
Had one FLUTE at least not been made into MAGIC!

SERIOUS HUMOUR

The clarinette, ancient in origin, now modernised
And ready for fresh ears to hear, maybe mesmerised,
First blown by that bloke who'd devised it with skill,
Of such-like concertos supremest stays still;
While others for oboe, flute, harp, horn, bassoon,
Composed he when not playing the silly buffoon!

If clean sounds his music, his letters by dozen
Were seen as obscene by some friends and one cousin.
Such letters as edited, readers are asked to risk
Those rude words ruled out, or marked with an asterisk.
He'd perpetrate puns too appalling to put up with
And part of his fun lay in phrases alliterative.

His "Musical Joke" although seriously written
Has bits which resemble bold Benjamin Britten,
A man whose main mania was Mozart and tennis,
Who raised a rare racket, then found where his pen is.
Tchaikowski and Beethoven, styles poles apart,
Like many more, made as their model our Mozart.

His young head contained in its uppermost attics
An uncanny aptitude towards mathematics,
While languages seemed to present him no problem,
Whenever confronted, he'd easily absorb them.
Wrote operas German, plus some in Italian,
Went French when in Paris, but Latin his Requiem.

Of five-staved note-paper he daily would fill yards;
In spare time he'd none of, he'd stoop to playing billiards,
Though "no time" to travel, he journeyed as far as
Such places as Prague, Rome, Linz, London and Paris.
Child-prodigy pianist, adept playing the fiddle,
He faced life's facts fully while flouting each riddle.

STORM AND STRUGGLE

He studied his musical forbears with reverence
Once, listening intently, his memory paid deference
To one called Allegri whose famed "Misereri"
No mortal might copy, yet Mozart, - how dare he! -
Amazed all of Rome plus the Vatican too
By rôte wrote each note! "See vat I can do!"

Delighting in orchestras large when available,
When not, he would write in a manner as amiable.
For quintets, quartets, trios, duos, works single,
Or bid bands of woodwinds in harmony mingle.
Though pouring out primarily an output quite secular,
His first post required of him Sacred-Works regular.

Quite adult in childhood, angelic in temperament,
Whiles childish in adult life; oft-times his temper meant
He'd quarrel with quacks who would quell his quaint crazes,
But true to his trade, he'd send critics to blazes.
Some dis-missed his dissonances, saying they were horrid,
While others insisted his style was too florid.

Too florid, like Salzburg's Cathedral in style,
Where Master of Music he'd been for a while.
Kicked out by an Archbishop called Coloredo,
Who acted in contrast to calling and Credo.
That kick, if it left that cruel cleric's leg lame,
Caused Mozart to move into fresh fields of fame!

He landed in Vienna where music he'd dish up
From off his own bat, *not* for bullying Archbishop,
Yet, far from aversion to true realms religious,
He mastered his C-minor Mass, - most prestgious,
Then later his Requiem, his last and his best,
But left it unfinished to take timeless rest.

TECHNICAL PERFECTION

What unusual finish, that unfinished masterpiece,
He called on his pupil Sussmayer from his class to piece
His notes and instructions together, - for lying
Gravely ill was his master, creatively dying,
While "Flauto Magico" to Opera-House packed
Was each night performed, - wild applause for each act!

In fact "Magic Flute" was *not* his last opera;
From comic to serious may perhaps have seemed properer.
"Clemenza di Tito" came next in due order
As though he liked one work on t'other to border;
When too busy piecing some great work together
He'd still squeeze another beside it as brother!

But back to his techniques with all their skilled counterpoint, -
A technical term which intends to surmount the point
That melodies mix with each other and mingle
Like webs spun by spiders from strands that are single, -
As such was the skill of each musical forefather,
Like Handel, and Bach whom he loved as his own father.

Their techniques would tend to transmit their complexity
To masterly writing all packed with much density
Ensuring each chorus or movement symphonic
Resounded concordant with sound polyphonic.
Such quality counts in creations supernal
Preserving their greatness to life all eternal.

Invaluable virtue for each virtuoso
Was Mozart's to vaunt with much verve, and we know so.
He rendered recitals to which they'd invite all
Enthusiasts musical, so to unite all
From far and from wide, assembled to witness
This keyboard-controller of fabulous fitness, -

RECITAL IN LEIPZIG

Like Leipzig, a city wherein they would write a list
Of persons prepared to perform as recitalist.
Good heavens! Old Bach had performed there for years!
This time was his church packed to give Mozart cheers,
Reciting with skill upon that same organ.
The whole town next day would wish him "Gut' Morgen!"

But though he had thrashed-out on keyboard and pedals
Such sounds as are sought-out by whoever meddles
With pipes, key-boards, stops, or some studies by Bach,
Young Mozart (who never grew old) just said "Ach!
I'll improvise now with no pre-written note."
Yet once for an organ of clockwork he wrote!

The paradox being that, despite such restriction,
That masterpiece since earned the highest distinction (Fantasia
As being of his best! But where does one draw   in F-minor)
The line between one form of musical law
And others which flout every lawful design?
But Mozart unblinking would say, "Well, it's mine!"

Now, what was his speciality? Piano Concertos? -
In which he'd play solo, and add his cadenzas, -
Or several symphonies, seven so sublime,
Beheld as being quite unsurpassed for all time.
True! Later ones use forces larger and stronger;
But quality, not quantity, tends to last longer.

There's music for many wind-instruments, strings,
Harmonica of glass, amongst other odd things!
Of Operas many of various titles,
Enacted on stage, sometimes sung at recitals,
Had only but ONE of those works been revived
Their composer would still at the top have survived!

LUX PERPETUA LUCEAT MOZART

Survives he more widely than ever before,
His name being well-known the wide world all o'er.
A snow-storm concealed where his corps lay at last,
And even his features as cast in a mask
Just crumbled to bits, - so symbolic, ensuring
That what matters most is his music enduring.

It seems sad for Mozart no chance would arrive
To hear his last symphonies (three) while alive.
May such masterpieces long live-on sublime
In Heaven's light bathed to perpetually shine.
Should Mozart have just fallen short of divinity,
Who knows, but his Person is "Fourth of the Trinity"!

NO, NO, NO! - to NAPOLEON

(AS ABANDONED BY BEETHOVEN)

A concert to mark an important occasion
Was foisted on French folk by powers of that nation
To honour Napoleon whose great anniversary
Observed by the French, is ignored universally.
His great works they worshipped, yet gave him the elbow
By sending him off to the Island of Elba.

Some said it was strange that Symphony Nine
Appeared on the programme as laid on the line
For Beethoven to honour the name of Napoleon
When one wished the other be boiled in hot oleum!
Napoleon at one time as hero he hailed,
But Symphony-Three had one movement unveiled . .

As Funeral March for that final event
When off in his coffin eventually sent.
The moment Napoleon declared himself Emperor,
Indignantly Beethoven quite lost his temper, for
In furious fits of a great righteous rage
He tore into bits the first title-page

Of famous "Eroica" - Symphony Three!
No more was Napoleon dedicatee. -
"Of good music wasted upon a dictator
I no longer wish to be proud dedicator!
Already I've written in mood of mad ferment
The funeral march for his final interment!"

And thus the Slow Movement of Symphony Three
Has ever since sounded most melanchol-ee
In contrast to great number Nine's "Ode to Joy"
Which would have pleased more that ebullient boy
Napoleon, . . who finally found his fate proven
Predicted in music by Ludwig Beethoven!

NAPOLEON SELF-STYLED EMPEROR
(NAPOLEON BONAPARTE 1769 - 1821)

Napoleon, who had declared himself Emperor, had no difficulty in acknowledging his own greatness. But he had seemingly gone just too far, and so was obliged to accept the wishes of those who decided that enough was enough. They banished him to the Island of Elba just across the water from Corsica (Corse in French) where he was born, and where they fed him with small tinned fish from the neighbouring island of Sardinia, having first set aside the bony part. Legend has it that, on arriving at Elba, he admitted that an end had come at last to the reign of power he had for so long enjoyed. So what did he say? Say this out loud, Children:-

"ABLE WAS I ERE I SAW ELBA."

Then get your parents to read this same quotation backwards, out loud, and ask yourself if you notice a certain similarity. If you do, ask them if they believe it a fact or not that Napoleon ever said such a thing. Answer below:-

---

Not true! Napoleon did not speak English!

AN OPERETTA BEHIND THE SCENES

One peep behind the theatre-curtain's quite inadequate
For scenes behind the scenes, hide yet more scenes from sight.
From several skills, from every walk of life, all ages,
Musicians, actors, acrobats, progress by STAGES,
Scene-painters, costume-makers, men who work the curtains,
Some hid from sight entirely, - combine in all the workings.

ADVANCE REHEARSALS

At first, the various sections quite separately rehearse
The ACTORS learn their lines as penned in prose or verse,
The SINGERS stretch their vocal chords in melodies
Committing all to storage in their memories.
While DANCERS pace their steps in measured pattern,
Conforming to the beat of the CONDUCTOR's baton.

PRODUCER

The show's PRODUCER must know every move by heart
Together with team-leaders works extremely hard,
Co-ordinates the work of ORCHESTRA placed in the pit
With that of LADIES making sure the costumes fit,
Plus those who work the LIGHTING, footlights, floods, and spots;
Though firm of brain and brawn, of tact must he have lots.

LIBRETTO

Now, long before the stage-production's even thought-of
Some rhymer or SCRIPT-WRITER must have thought a lot of
Lines up, for some competent COMPOSER skilled
Enough to have his verbiage with music filled,
So that it sounds a lot less dreadful, maybe better,
Presented as an OPERA, - or operetta.

COMPOSER

The music set to each libretto, as you know, sir!
Has long-since been, or just been set by great composer.
But think-you that his vocal and orchestral score
Had just been thought-up p'raps a night or two before?
Unless his name were Mozart, no sir! for at pains he was
For months or even years to make it sound spontaneous!

COSTUMES

Some made-up new, some hired for this production specially
Must all be laid-out in the wardrobe-room expressly,
Befitting all who sing in chorus, act, or dance.
Oh what a job-of-work well thought-out in advance!
A ladies powder-room, plus dressing-room for gents,
Are supplemented by a pressing-room for pants.

WARDROBE-LADIES

One section's set aside, essential so it seems
For several needle-wielders set on sewing seams
All stitching busily, at sewing-machines they sit.
Ensuring actively that actors' costumes fit.
"Excuse us, gentlemen and ladies, we must beg
Your pardon as we measure-up your inside-leg."

DANCING DAMSELS

Young girls with supple sylph-like figures all elastic
A-dancing daintily on tip-toe, light, fantastic,
Have long-since practised skilful steps and movements gracious
And now the day has dawned to flaunt their forms curvacious.
And even men who meant to take up ballet-dancing
Look much less ugly by the make-up-stick's enhancing.

THE MAKE-UP DEPARTMENT

Pink rouge, red lipstick, eye-brow-shadow, for the stage
Can make those men and women look just half their age.
For make-up plus those stage-lights tend to hide the wrinkles . . !
Now wake-up, hasten to the scene. The stage-bell tinkles!
Hush-hush! as the CONDUCTOR paces to his podium
Holds high his baton, as the audience starts applauding him.

CURTAIN OPEN

The Overture commences, complete with crashing chords;
The curtain-raisers wait to pull the curtain-cords,
The music as melodious as anyone could wish,
That Overture now over, sure the curtains part, swish-swish!
The splendid scene's revealed; - the audience enraptured
Commends those sights all thrilled, they'd not till now encaptured.

PROPPING-UP THE PROPERTIES

Yet let us not forget, before those scenes were painted,
Those men we'd never met, - with joiner-work acquainted,
Who'd formed the scenery by sawing, hammering hard,
In readiness for scenes being painted yard by yard.
Mere optical illusions look so realistic!
With artistry by scenic-painters so artistic!

UNFINISHED FINALE

Where are they all? Why be those artists sadly lacking
Who humbly hidden, yet have propped-up all the acting?
Unseen by all the audience as they clap their paws
While, lined-up for their credits, all others get applause.
The orchestra remember, down in the pit below,
Together with each member who made that memorable show!

GREAT MUSIC
A FUND OF FUNDAMENTAL FUN

Great Music, often classed as Classical,
(Convenient name by which to class it all,)
Exists in many different forms and fashions
Emotional feelings, sadness, amorous passions,

Humorous, soothing, loving, mind-improving,
Drifting, shifting, mind-uplifting, moving.
But very oft forgotten is the fact
That much is full of **FUN**, with wit all packed.

VERY NECESSARY PREFACE
to COMMENTS CONCERNING COMPOSERS

A LITTLE REFLECTION SHOULD CONFIRM THE FACT THAT OUR GREAT COMPOSERS ARE ENDOWED WITH SOME OF THE MOST HIGHLY DEVELOPED INTELLECTS AND AESTHETIC PERCEPTIONS THIS WORLD HAS EVER KNOWN.

MANY MASTERPIECES ARE POSSESSED OF AN INGENUITY AND STRUCTURAL COMPLEXITY QUITE UNSURPASSED IN ANY OTHER MEDIUM.

AS GREAT CATHEDRALS ARE SOUNDLY BUILT, SO GREAT SYMPHONIES ARE BUILT OF SOUND.

THE MEANS BY WHICH SUCH MASTER-WORKS ARE PRESENTED DOES NOT DEPEND UPON ACCOUSTIC AMPLIFICATION, BUT RELIES UPON THE CO-ORDINATION OF SOMETIMES LARGE NUMBERS OF HIGHLY TRAINED AND HIGHLY EXPERIENCED PERFORMERS AND CONDUCTORS.

THE GENIUS OF GREAT COMPOSERS COMES FROM GOD KNOWS WHERE, - AND *ONLY* GOD KNOWS WHERE, - AS MANY COMPOSERS AGREE.

THE RATHER FACETIOUS COMMENTS THAT FOLLOW ARE NOT INTENDED AS AN INSULT TO THE GREAT MASTERS, BUT RATHER AS AN ACKNOWLEDGEMENT THAT THEY TOO REALISE:

A LITTLE NONSENSE NOW AND THEN
IS RELISHED BY THE WISEST MEN!

COMMENTS on COMPOSERS
TAKE ONE AT A TIME. DO NOT EXCEED THE STATED DOSE.

LET JOHANN SEBASTIAN BACH
HAVE THE FIRST AND LAST WORD
(THIS ONE IS BASED ON DOCUMENTED FACT)

Of Well-Tempered Bach it is told
That he once lost the head, which got cold
    As he flung off his wig
    Both hairy and big
At a tenor he needed to scold.

He whizzed that big wig with directitude
At that tenor of tonal ineptitude!
    One notes many men are
    Of un-even tenor,
So the wigging laid bare his true attitude!

Said one of his orchestral violins,
Reproaching old Bach for his violence,
    "Keep your hair on! That wig-thing
    Sheds Hair-on-the-G-String!"
Bach put him behind bars . . of silence.

FROM RUSSIA

Great Russian Romantic Tchaikowski
Went to bed with a cold and rough cough-ski,
    But his doctor attending
    He kept on offending
For Tchaikowski just coughed-out "Buzz-off-ski!"

No rival in Russia worth talking-of
Existed until Rimsky-Korsakov
    Began to compose
    As one would suppose
Once Rimsky of course ripped his corsets off.

The coffee they'd proffered Prokoviev
Was brought in a box bought in North-Kiev
    Where coffee for quaffing
    Would cost next to nothing
If you'd coppers enough to cough-up with.

Some folk think Stravinsky was awful
With no right to spring things as novel
    As that frightful thing
    He called "Rite of Spring"
But he thought such folk talked only waffle.

FROM GERMANY AND AUSTRIA

Now, what would old Bach or old Handel
Have thought of such musical scandal?
    They'd scan each edition
    With deep erudition,
But just find them too hard to handle.

Some symphonies people decide on
Composed best by old Joseph Haydn,
    Just made Haydn sick
    Of playing hide-and-seek
With his notes till the day that he died on.

He tried being un-beaten by Beethoven
A bit more off-beat, as is proven,
    His hunger oft stated
    Symphonically sated
And by buns he baked hot in his great oven.

Franz Schubert bumped into Rob Schumann
And hailed him as unusually human,
    By saying, "So it's you, Bert!"
    As Schumann said, "Schubert!"
With Schubert assuming, "It's you, man!"

When Schubert had duly departed
And off in his coffin got carted,
    His final work written
    In heaven for certain
Is commonly called 'The Unstarted.'

Too romantic was Johannes Brahms
Said a girl wriggling free from his arms;
    "In future, Johannes,
    Just keep your two hannes
To yourself, whatever my charms."

Karl, Freischutz, Maria von Weber
Had made his most musical labour
    The work he'd found fun with,
    Once Oberon done with,
His Overtures all Europe could savour

Dick Wagner created much din;
Some love it, some think it's a sin.
    Of lady-friends numerous
    Not many were humorous,
Just once he made one Low-hen-grin!

Franz Liszt of the rarest of species
Kept pounding his piano to pieces
    Playing preludes for palming off
    On great Serge Rachmanninov
Who more than kept up with his paces.

Though Burns once expressed 'To a Mouse'
How he felt as that mouse fled her house
    In agonised prancing,
    She much preferred dancing
To the waltzes of Strauss' "Fledermaus".

The German-born Strauss known as Richard
Found music complex not a bit hard
    While turning folk-poems
    To orchestral tone-poems
Un-Till Eulenspiegel was featured.

Not one note in five-hundred thousand
Sufficed for a chap called Stockhausen
    Whose sonic effects
    Seemed cronic defects
To his wife. So he'd not let his spouse in.

The Mother of Anthony Bruckner
Kept many a musical book on her
    High shelves in Vienna,
    That her son in his manner
Might transpose that quizzical look on her.

Great Symphonies, - the lengthiest yet,
Came from Mahler, - full TEN of a set,
    Received much ovation
    Except in that nation
Which suffered from Mahler-la-Tête!

Karl Orf charged off one manjana
To write his "Carmina Burana"
    Saying, 'Time that I left here,'
    So pulled from his left ear
His deaf-aid, - a yellow banana!

FROM FRANCE

A fellow from France, just as charming,
When working too hard, saw no harm in
    Saying, 'Carl Orf, I'm Bizet,
    Charge off, I'm too busy
Composing my Opera "Carmen".

Frank Poulenc, amusing composer,
Was right up to date, as you know, sir,
    While ancient styles choosing
    With brand new ones fusing,
Liked 'Pullink' your leg I suppose, sir?

Further Frenchmen one often hears tell o'
Debussy, and Maurice Ravel, oh!
    Each fine French Impressionist
    Wrote much to impress you with:
La Mer, La Valse, and Bolero.

"For feeding my favourite French pussy,
A tin of 'Kit-Kat' j'ai re-ussi
    In daily dispatching
    To keep it from scratching."
Or else had de cat Clawed Debussy!

Some songs as suggested by Chausson
For singing 'comme beaucoup plus beaux chants'
    Though seldom one's sure
    Should one sing in chaussures,   (shoes)
Or sing solely in slippers, or chaussons?

Some songs set for singing by Saint-Saens
Seem specially for saints set on dansant,
    That song, "All the Saints" is,
    As Vaughan Williams paints it,
Supreme in a series of saints-songs.

FROM ENGLAND

Composer of unusual brilliance
Whose 'Folk-Song-Suite's well-known to millions
    Wrote Symphonies nine,
    All fabulously fine
As fashioned by famed Ralph Vaughan Williams.

He said, as he met Jean Sibelius,
'It gives me great pleasure to hail you as
    Fine friend to the Finnish!
    May you never diminish
As foremost of Finland's non-failures.'

Preceded by Elgar the Edwardian
Whose repute grew into a large one
    First found recognition
    Abroad, - till his nation
At last pulled him in from the margin.

No notes had for Bretons been written
By Britisher Benjamin Britten,
    For had he but writ any
    Not quite fit for Brittany,
They'd have bundled Ben Brit back to Britain.

He'd based his good taste upon Purcell,
Tasted many a musical morsel,
    Invariably composed
    In freshly-washed clothes
With the aid of a packet of Persil.

William Walton, a Lancashire lad,
Wrote much from which pleasure be had
    His Belshazzar's Feast
    By no means his least,
Is much more than just a Façade.

ITALY   HUNGARY   POLAND

Italianate sunshine and song
Still shine since Rossini was born
    As Overture-maker
    Opera creator,
A pleasure to act and perform.

Joe Verdi wrote always with every ease
Being energised largely by elbow-grease,
    Till a sculptor, Nabucco,
    Who modelled in stucco,
Had plastered his hair with green Verdi-gris.

A hairless composer named 'Baldy'
Asked red-haired Antonio Vivaldi,
    "Please, please, Pre-te Rosso,
    Compose 'piu mosso'!
Said Tony, 'Si, si, Fresco-Baldi.'

More up-to-date Signor Respighi
Loved tunes of old-times, and indeed he
    Brought much up to date
    Each night working late
On Fountains of Rome, Prima Vera, - till midi.

That Polish Composer Fred Chopin
Was poles apart from Beethoven
    While shoppin' around
    For lost Chords, he found
One that Mendelssohn gave him for nothin'.

Two fellows for music being hungry
Based much on the folk-songs of Hungary
    One, Bartok, caused fiddles
    Play musical riddles,
While Kodaly made listeners less angry.

CZECHOSLOVAKIA   AMERICA

Few Britains had heard tell of Janacek
Until Walter Susskind (that man a Czech)
    To Scotland endeared him   (Glasgow & Edinburgh
    Where loudly they cheered him,   circa 1947)
And generously handed the man a cheque.

How sad that the sweet spouse of Smetana
Expired from a bug that had smitten her;
    A rare influenza
    Had dared influence her
All due to a dip in the Ultava.

That 'Old World' of Czechoslovakia
Was Dvorãk's, who fortunes turned luckier
    Once over the Ocean.
    Then harboured the notion
Of Czeching if he could get back there . . .

From New World, America, where
New music is made, to compare
    With Old World tradition,
    While men like George Gershwin
Had ideas with others to share.

In mixing of styles, great George Gershwin
To JAZZ showed no undue aversion;
    His Rhapsodies too
    Were baptised in blue
Once surfaced from total immersion.

Aaron Copland, Len Bernstein, Sam Barbour
Plus many more names one could harbour,
    Thus going on for ever,
    More flippant than clever;
Than the few listed here, there are far more.

PART 8

LITERARY LAMENTATIONS
AND RHYMING FOR FUN

1. SERIOUS SIN

2. APOLOGY FOR PUNS?

3. MODERN VERSE

4. THE LIMITS OF LIMERICKS

5. THE LAWS OF LIMERICKS

6. THE BISHOP'S CROSSWORD

7. STRANGE-SOUNDING NAMES

8. STRANGE-SOUNDING PLACES

9. LAMENTABLE LIMERICKS

SERIOUS SIN

So sad was the lad who said levity
Was a serious form of depravity
For he would do well,
To learn Satan fell
Into hell by the full force of gravity.

FOOTNOTE: THAT UNIVERSALLY CELEBRATED POET KNOWN AS
ROBERT BURNS, WHOSE PHENOMENAL VERSATILITY OF STYLE
ENCOMPASSED THE DEEPEST EXPRESSIONS OF PATHOS, VENTURED
ALSO INTO THE REALMS OF THE HIGHLY AMUSING. IN THE LAST
LINE OF ONE OF HIS VERSIFIED EPISTLES, DID HE PROCLAIM QUITE
SIMPLY, "I RHYME FOR FUN!"

APOLOGY FOR PUNS?

ROBERT SERVICE: 1874 - 1958

Be assured, - on the painful pursuance of puns,
In many famed authors that old ailment runs,

For old William Shakespeare could always suggest-a-pun,
As also (and often) would Gilbert K Chesterton!

There's Belloc, Lew Carrol, and Sam Taylor-Coleridge,
While Yeatman and Sellars wrote "Ten-Sixty-Six", they did.

Quite punintentionally would old Thomas Hood
Hoodwink you by punning whenever he could.

Though Oliver Goldsmith had no puns inserted
He just left them out, like a Village, - Deserted.

Of my personal propensity I blow no loud trumpet,
While those who don't like it can jolly-well lump it!

MODERN VERSE GETS WORSE

IN RESPONSE TO MR STEPHEN FRY'S RECENT OUTCRY IN THE
OBSERVER, - AN OBSERVER'S OBSERVATIONS HEREWITH:

Young posers "poetic" don't try
To rhyme in their writings, - just why?
    Not rhythmically even
    Nor rhyming says Stephen!
They *should* be, - or else they must FRY!

The Dictionary, however, proposes
That "poetry" may proceed from proses
    So high elevated
    As may be equated
To poetry which rhymes, - one supposes?

The art of poetic tradition
Being high above prosaic fashion
    Has strict laid-down rules
    Ignored by such fools
As think they're above that position.

FOOTNOTE: RULES ARE OFTEN HONOURED IN
THE BREACH RATHER THAN IN THE OBSERVANCE.

THE LIMITS OF LIMERICKS

A lady allergic to limericks,
Alleged they were built-up by silly tricks
    All limited largely
    To word-play, and hardly
Worth building in Lego or Minibrix.

FOOTNOTE: HERE FOLLOWETH SOME OF THE
WORST LIMERICKS EVER WRITTEN, PREFACED,
HOWEVER BY A SET OF STRICT RULES TO BE
OBSERVED WHEN TRYING TO WRITE THEM.

LAYING DOWN THE
LAWS OF LIMERICKS

All verses which rhyme must have metre
Insisted a poet called Peter
    Who always kept with him
    Some measure of rhythm
So joined a jazz-band as drum-beater.

A regular rhymster called Dan
Writes verses which simply won't scan.
    Each verse he invents
    Displays his attempts
To cram as much polysyllabic verbosity
    into his last lines as he
    possibly can!

But Patrick, a young Irish bard,
Found metric verse somewhat too hard.
    'My meter's for gas',
    Said he, so alas!
He measured his metres in yards.

A potty old poet from Kerse
Wrote quite unintelligible verse,
    And just to be awkward
    Wrote every word backward
Interspersed with each verse in reverse.

A learned professor called Spooner
Caused quite uninhensional tumour
    By his habit to hack words
    Turned frowards to backwards
When occasions the least opportune are.

An impediment meant in his chatter
What he said he meant didn't much matter
    For later or sooner
    We'd all be, said Spooner
As clay in the ponds of the hatter!

There was a young man from Dundee
Who got stung on his neck by a wasp,
    Said the doctor in hospital,
    T'was a bee, not a wasp at all',
Such stings he'd distinguish in-sting-tively.

THE BISHOP'S CROSSWORD
PLUS SOME WORDS THAT GOT CROSSED

KNOCK-KNOCK!
    "Who's there?" enquired old Bishop Riley.
"The boy, my Lord," replied his servant shyly.
"Ah! Do come in, - I have a question, Frazer,
Concerns my crossword, just one question-raiser."
Young Frazer bowed, inclined his ear politely;
He'd come about the lap-top-lunch he'd serve directly.

    "One word, - four letters, ending in I - T?
I've only sketched it in, thank God Almighty!"
The servant-boy attentive standing by
Made bold to ask the Bishop ere reply,
"And what would be the crossword clue, my Lord?
It may just be I have the very word!"

    "It says, 'hm, 'Found upon a bird-cage floor'."
"Of course," said Frazer, - "Let me close the door, -
'The bottom of a bird-cage' - must be 'G R I T'!"
The bishop glared at what he just had writ.
"Ah, Frazer! Frazer jolly-good-fellow! Frazer!
Now, could you lend me your eraser, Frazer?"

    Then off went Frazer to the household kitchen,
"His Lordship's lunch not ready yet to fetch in?"
Unluckily for him, he put his foot in it, -
No, not the lunch, - but words that wouldn't fit.
He'd been a student at the school of Spooner
Whose habits he'd inherit, late or sooner.

As infant, Frazer's Ma spoon-fed him with
A sticky syrup he grew fed-up with
Not just because his pair of sticky lips
Got stuck with stuff she *would* call 'Haws and Hips',
Thus going against all verbal laws, - but 'cause
She really should have called it 'Hips and Haws'.

"Be you still kizzy in the bitchen, Lizzie?
Still oiling your old bunions? seems you're busy,
One half-formed wish still prying in the fan,
While you, half-done, still stoving at the stand,
Still cook that snack to lace before his Plordship?
Now lettuce get a move-on, his lord to Please-ship!"

"Meanwhile, I'm off to boil my icicle
Because the Bean's too dizzy to de-ice it all.
He comes by bus by way of Byford Watpass,
Right turning on the first, he'll thravel turd-class.". . .
By which time Frazer'd grown a little older,
His deepening voice had grown a great deal bolder,

Yet still he got his verbiage confused
To which old habit folk had long got used.
"At last! - a most malicious deal to dish-up!
It's pure to sleaze my beer-old Dish the Lordshop!"
KNOCK-KNOCK! - "Whose there?" enquired old Bishop Riley,
"THE LORD, MY BOY," said Frazer, grinning widely.

STRANGE-SOUNDING NAMES

TO NAME A PERSON OR A PLACE
   IN MANNER NORMALLY ACCEPTED
ANOMALIES ONE HAS TO FACE
   OR ONE MAY STAND TO BE CORRECTED
SOME PROBLEMS OF PRONUNCIATION
DEPEND ON ONE'S ENUNCIATION.

An author called Evelyn Waugh   ('Wauch' in Scotland)
In Scotland tried laying down the law
   That his name be announced
   As in England pronounced,
But the Scots had him chucked in the LOCH

He met there a fellow called Menzies   ('Mingis' in Scotland)
About whom the peculiar thing is
   He incessantly chatters
   Irrelevant matters
So works himself up into frenzies.

A laddie called Daniel Dalzell   ('Dyell' in Scotland)
Was asked by one of his palls, 'Well,
   Do tell us just why
   Your 'Z's pronouned 'Y',
He said he had told them, but had 'e 'ell!

At school we used to smile wryly
On a fellow whose name was Jack Smellie   ('Smyllie' in
    Fed-up, he arranged   Scotland)
    To have his name changed,
So came up with his new name. - George Smellie.

The English just cannot say 'Murdoch',
To Scots no more hard than the word 'Och'!
    To get round their problem -
    May the good Lord absolve them -
They murder the name mouthed as 'Meudock'!

The way we say La*MONT* or *LA*mont
With studious care be examined
    If French or Ecossais
    Just comme je prononce est
Vari-é in odd parts of le monde.

The topic in newspapers raged
As some people felt quite enraged
    Names change as they wear old,
    Claimed a scribe in the HERALD
However they're printed or paged.

STRANGE-SOUNDING PLACES

(WITH FAR-AWAY NAMES)

A Scotsman who'd roamed from his clachan
To England, declared his name 'Strachan'
    But, fed-up called 'Strawn'
    Set both feet upon
German soil, and settled in Aix-la-Chapelle.   (AACHEN)

Not far off from Glasgow, Milngavie
Is pronounced by the locals, 'Mulguy'
    Like Ireland's Dun Laoghaire
    Best known as 'Dunleary'. . .
Dan Leary? - a weary old navvy?

A laddie who lived in Cholmondeley
Loved his lassie uncommonly fondly
    But turned quite un-chumly
    As *she* called it Chumley
Pronouncing their home-town so rumly.

'Please tell me the way to Wor-cester?'
'What, Chester? Oh, don't you mean Towcester?'
    'No, no, it's near Toaster,
    Perhaps its called Wooster,
Or Doncs'ter, or Dawster, spelt Dorchester.'
    (And, if you insist, then Cirnster is Cirencester)

PREFACE IN PROSE TO
A LIMITED LIST OF LIMERICKS

A LIMERICK does not really have to make sense, and rarely does. To serve its purpose, it must sound right, and thus have a musical value. If based on alliteration, so much the better, especially for children who may also find entertainment in conquering the challenges of tongue-twisters. Hence they can profit from exercises in elocution. Rude limericks are by no means rare, and are said to be the best ones, but space, perhaps a modicum of discretion, forbids their inclusion herein.

The prolific list of existing limericks goes on for ever. Those appearing herein are either original, or derived from those overheard, but never actually seen in print, in which case apologies are proffered to their unknown originators, no doubt long since gone to their reward. But their spirit lives on in the lyrics of their limericks.

Read on. It is time for rhyme.

A LIST OF ALLITERATIVE TONGUE-TWISTERS

NOW TRY THESE OUT ON YOUR CHILDREN!

To this day the mystery thickens!
One wonders why old Charlie Dickens,
    Inexplicably quick in
    The right nick-name picking,
Picked 'Pickwick' the big-wig, - the dickens!

Two lassies from quite cultured classes
Required each a case for her glasses.
    "Sir, any respectable
    Spectacle-receptacle's
Acceptable to us classie lassies."

No tame toad could totally tire
Of his twin-toad in two-toned attire
    As main modern modes
    Are twain-tones for toads
Or twins of tame toads to acquire.

Your hot-water-bottle don't throttle,
But properly stop with a stopper, -
    More probably proper
    To stopper that bottle
And bottom the bottle with copper.

The snuff-shop of Sam sold such stuff
As he stocked on his shelves, - just enough
    Strong stuff fit for whiffing
    As folk fixed on sniffing
Slipped into his shop to sniff snuff.

The last block of butter that Betty bought
Went bad as it sat in the butter-pot!
    So Betty had better
    Buy much better butter
Than last lot, - an utterly bitter lot!

A frog in Fred's throat! Fred felt rough!
For that frog was uncomfortably tough.
    For fear he'd froget
    Frogs frequently fret
Fred forced the frog out with a cough.

A big boy, Bill Blake, - not a bad bloke, -
Bought a bike, but bits from its back broke,
    For badly by accident
    He had his back axle bent,
And broken was Bill Blake's back brake-block.

Of Roderick Brodrick one often talks
Of growing a gross lot of rotten crops,
    So, cropping the lot
    Of his tropical crop,
He opted for tall crops of hollihocks.

A fly and a flea in a flue
Knew not what each other should do
    Said the fly, 'Let us flee!'
    Said the flea, 'Let us fly!'
So they flew through a flaw in the flue.

Remember young Michelle from Seychelles?
She excels in her selling of sea-shells.
    She still sells, we're sure,
    From Seychelles sea-shore
Such shells as seem special to Michelle.

ODD PEOPLE DO ODD THINGS

A lady who'd long lived in Cheltenham
Tried shoes on to see how she felt in 'em,
    But, trotting to Tottenham,
    Her feet grew so hot in 'em
That her toes and heels started to melt in 'em.

In the Cinema, Simon had seen a man
Suck sticks of a substance called cinamon;
    But a young usherette
    To his utter regret
Said, "Your cinamon-limit's a minimum."

The cucumber-crop grown at Kew
Too cumbersome grew for old Hugh
    Who cut down in number
    His crop of cucumber
To encumber himself with but few.

A seller of salt, Sally Keller,
Stored sacks of such salt in her cellar.
    The salt one could savour
    In only one flavour,
"That's saline", said Sally, salt-seller.

That eligible lass called Susanne
Cooked edible food in Lausanne
    Served all over Switzerland,
    Ever since known as Pizza-land,
Now famed for its lovely Lasagne.

Four fellows from far-off Strathpeffer,
So stupidly sniffing black pepper,.
    Soon sensed that such sniffing-stuff
    Should suffice to send them off
All sneezing together to Chester.

A young girl called Valerie Lunn
Was chewing a high-calorie bun.
    For some obscure reason
    She choked on a raisin,
Then boaked, which she didn't find fun.

A half-crazy crack-pot from Crew
Held high his sledge-hammer to do
    What a nut might expect,
    But all that he cracked
Was the haft of his hammer in two!

Young Laura, that loveliest of lassies,
Lost all her long lovely eye-lashes
    For that lively young wire
    Fell flat in the fire
Till little was left but her ashes!

A Frenchman with bizarre opinions
Ate mushrooms served up with raw onions,
    But one day that old fool
    Died, - eating a toadstool!
Why hadn't he champed on champignons?

That mad man named Dan from Manhattan
Had sat on my chair with my hat on
    Thus crushing my hat
    Like a pancake quite flat.
"Thanks Dan, that's *my* hat you've sat on!"

A male owl who simply said, "Coo!"
To a young lady-owl whom he knew
    Turned out as no match for her
    So stayed as a bachelor
By lacking enough wit to woo!

All portions of pork Jews refuse;
Quite rightly they pick and they choose,
    And prefer lamb or beef,
    To a piggy's relief,
So pigs never pick upon Jews!

There once was a fellow from Sydney
Who suffered from pains in the kidney,
    So he prayed to the Lord
    That he'd have him restored,
And he promised he would, - but he didnae!

A chap champing food in Botswana
Once choked as he chewed a banana
    In which rather urgent state
    He tried to regurgitate
But only brought back a sultana!

A fellow from far-away Fotheringham
Whose brother would never stop bothering him
    Just pressed a soft pillow
    On the face of the fellow
With the honourable object of smothering him!

A vexatious vixen from Exeter
Felt vexed as men stretched rubber necks at her
    With salacious suggestions
    Of lecherous intentions
As they sexily stared through their specs at her.

Prunella who'd prudently pruned
Several plums once her plum-tree had bloomed
    Was sure she had swallowed
    Such prunes, for they followed
Their course through her tubes till she swooned.

An old man who hailed from Hillhead
Preferred being interred when quite dead
    In accord with his will
    At the top of the hill,
But he slid down to Hillfoot instead.

(Both places are districts of Glasgow, - one not far from its
centre, the other, complete with cemetery, in its outskirts. The
saying goes that people live to die in one, and are dying to live
in the other.)

In choosing one's words to perfection
One use's one's verbal perception,
    But poor Mrs Maladroit
    Would use words so malaprop
With great circumspect circumcision.

FROM BRITAIN TO BRITTANY

Les gens tous ensemble à Cézembre
Demandaient que pendant septembre
    On pense bien avant
    Le mois de novembre
Qu'on mange leur gingembre en décembre.

(Cézembre is a small island off the coast of Brittany from
which copious quantities of underground ginger may be mined
by the gullible.)

ENGLISH AS SHE IS SPOKE

(OR MAYBE MURDERED)

To the English, American sounds foul,
For such is the sound of each vowel.
    That Opera's called 'Apera'!
    What *could* be imprAperer?
Thyat's just wan ex*e*mple, nat Ahll!

To Scots, southern English is worse
Pronouncing some words most perverse
    Each letter 'R's missed-out,
    Yet where it exists not
The law-r of the letter's reversed!

While 'oop-North' they talk their words foonie
Just 'ear how the fawk pronounce 'hoonie'!
    They leave out their 'H'-es,
    As 'as 'appened for ages
While rolling thirr 'R'-s round and roonie.

The English of Scotland sounds best
When spoken in far Inverness,
    Each vow-el sounds pure,
    Each consonant sure
Of being soundly and clearly expressed.

To try standardise the world's accents
Would lack understanding, and lack sense.
    What matters is clarity
    Despite wide disparity;
Auld Scots wad agree that that maks sense!

PART 9

MATTERS OF LIFE AND DEATH
REGRETS, TRIBUTES TO THE GREAT

THE CAKE THAT GOES NOT STALE
(WITH A MODICUM OF VERNACULAR STIRRED IN)

We're a' doon here fur yin brief period
    Be one jist dense or clever,
Yet some fowk think it's very odd
    We dinnae last fur ever.

Should life seem jist a piece o'cake,
    At least oor current one,
Or jist mare like the bread we bake,
    Or else a currant bun,

Whate'er the case, a cake's a nice thing
    Maist bakers largely can
Enhance by topping wi' thin icing
    Or inch-thick marzipan . . .

Or fill the thing till full o' fruit,
    Thus fruitfully fulfilling
Its function fully absolute
    For fulsome faces filling.

One's cake, ye langer may conserve it if
    Ye hae the right stuff handy,
Jist add a guid preservative
    Perhaps a wee-bit brandy.

Though slim oor slice o' life, it's ample!
    Thin slice jist let it be.
We flourish till we're free to sample
    Life's lang eternity.

Oor life was ne'er a piece of cake,
    We've yet tae meet oor Maker.
But mind, - nae cake was ever baked
    That's greater than its baker!

Of ROSEMARY and ME

WHEN WE WERE VERY YOUNG

Our City of Glasgow, a grim and a large one,
Lay next to Clydebank's industrial margin,
    While knowing nothing different
    Dislike it we didn't,
Growing up where our parents had left us at large in.

The shipyards were clanging all day as they clattered,
For fixing to steel frames, the riveters battered
    Those steel sheets they'd wrought
    With rivets red-hot   *
To result in great ships - which vitally mattered,

But not to us kiddies, our noses all snotty,
Habitually playing in our back-lanes all grotty,
    While sounding our hooters
    We pushed our wee scooters
Regarding all adult-control as quite potty.

But being from a family parentally mixed,
Our holidays distant were annually fixed
    In far away Surrey
    Where no hectic hurry
Of city-life vexed us, - all seemed so relaxed.

Away from those shipyards, away from the bustling,
One scented the ROSE, one heard the birds whistling.
    So rural the scenery,
    Entranced by its greenery,
Of life's actual facts we knew not the first thing.

Tne first thing in fact that I noticed was ROSE,
My dear cousin Rose, - one wouldn't suppose
    When sent off discretely
    To bed, we completely
Divested ourselves of all of our clothes.

One feels, aged just four, no shame in being stripped,
"What's that little tap with which you're equipped?
    I'd love one of those"
    Sighed dear cousin Rose
"Why can't I have one of my own?" - she near wept!

Our race so divided! - just half have attached
Those things girls attach to, once finally matched.
    She acquired one in time,
    Someone else's, not mine!
It's fate that decides how romances are hatched.

Ah, Rose, my dear Rose, dear Rosemarie,
If life in eternity's supposed to be
    Of permanent bliss
    Then grant me just this:
One life-long liaison twixt dear Rose and me!

*   (AT THAT STAGE IN HISTORY, - THE ART OF WELDING
      HAD NOT YET REPLACED THE OLD ART OF RIVETING)

THE NAKED TRUTH REVEALED
Now that I'm very old

The bath I took unto myself this morning
Was quite without the slightest prior warning
Should pryers uninvited perhaps arrive at
The scene I'd happily prefer in private.

I did, - relaxed in water hot and soapy, - ah!
What luxury of life, what near Utopia!
Ignore the telephone, ignore all urgent
Demands when one just wallows in detergent.

But stepping out from that warm water so that
I might just dry myself stood on the bath-mat,
I cast a downward glance, Could I still hing
My bath-towel on that one-time useful thing?

No! Nowadays no towel can I suspend
On what droops down in one curvacious bend.
So sadly sags that flag-pole, - play-time past -
No flag can fly, not even at half-mast!

Of life now winding-down it seems symbolic;
One practises no more one's favourite frolic,
But while some time is left, be there some hope in it?
It may still slide in slowly with some soap on it!

MONK and MONSTER

Have you ever met a monk?
    One monk I know quite well.
Now value him amongst
    My best of friends as well.

First feeling rather timid in
    Imagining him formal,
Despite the garb he hid in
    I found him fully normal.

Did he possess the choice to
    Engage in conversation?
Ah! parted from his cloister,
    He'd talk without cessation!

Alone in that great Abbey, he
    Apart from me who crept in,
Was playing the organ happily
    Which he was most adept in.

I recognised the piece
    He practised with much skill,
Not wishing him to cease,
    Awaited its fin-ale.

"I know that fugue you've played"
    And whistled its fine theme,
He widely grinned and said,
    "I must begin again,

For sad, but true, the fact is
    I'm but an amateur,
So lacking in my practice
    That's but my overture."

An overture it proved
   For many times since then
We'd frequently been moved
   To chat, and chat again.

Our conversation turned
   From matters mainly musical,
To what he'd lately learned.
   "Do you have any news at all

About the famous monster - eh?
   No recent de-monster-ation
As seen nearby your monastery?"
   In mock-remonster-ation, . .

He said that he believed not
   In what had been alluring
Quite mythically, he grieved not,
   Those curious tourists touring.

They come here horde by horde;
   All ask that same old question,
I get a little bored
   But make the same suggestion:

"Consult the Abbey bookshop,
   There's all the gen within
All research to be looked up,
   Authentic, genuine."

I, personally, if you ask me,
   Think all is just a myth
I've seen it not, it just be
   For teasing tourists with."

But here, lest we digress,
    The place, to do it justice,
Lies right beside Loch Ness
    And known as Fort Augustus.

Loch Ness is deadly deep,
    Of fathomless profundity,
Within its waters creep
    Those creatures in fecundity.

Not one alone, for families
    Must surely reproduce
Or else they face calamities
    Like sliding out of use.

Their history is famous
    Going back by several centuries
Columba, Saint by name is,
    Invariably adventurous,

While standing on the banks,
    Had seen it showing off
Displaying its usual pranks,
    And told it to shove off.

He died five-ninety-seven,   (597 A.D.)
    Columba, not the monster,
And went straight up to heaven.
    The monster carried on, sir.

To get back to my Monk-friend
    Full fifteen years had passed
(The one who'd said, "It's bunk, friend.")
    We met again at last.

In mufti, incognito,
  He'd not be recognised
From far across the street, oh!
  But how he'd be surprised!

The tune by which I hailed him
  I whistled loud and clear
From t'other side of road,
  Amazed, it met his ear.

At once he recognised
  The tune he'd played of Bach,
Which caused him such surprise
  He crossed the road saying "Ach!

It's you again at last!
  You haven't changed your tune!
Since all that time has passed,
  The time seems opportune

To sit and reminisce,
  Let's have a cup of tea,
Of that affair and this." -
  A chatty chap was he.

Long time since I had heard
  In semi-secret session
That unbelieving word
  Of which he'd made confession.

"Since last time that I saw you,
  My mind I've changed completely;
The Monster, I assure you.
  Myself I've seen distinctly!

"While ambling by the Lochside
    Along with one eye-witness
Who strolled with me alongside
    And couldn't care a whit less

About that silly subject.
    Discussing other things
As was our aim and object . . .
    Quite suddenly, "**By jings!**"

Said he in terms un-muffled,
    For rising from the calm
Of Loch Ness quite un-ruffled,
    To our intense alarm

An unforseen emergency
    Arose! - A monster's head
Decided to emerge and see
    If it had been mis-led

Concerning *our* existence.
    It looked around inquisitive.
Then, at my friends insistence,
    We asked ourselves, "What *is* it if

It's not that very Nessie?"
    Its neck arose quite long,
Head swivelled round, I guess he
    Was wondering if we'd gone,

Then with a sudden swishing
    It dived below once more
Attending to its fishing,
    While we stayed on the shore.

We'd seen no false illusion,
    We'd drunk no alcohol,
And lest there be confusion,
    We'd not been drunk at all.

Completely realistic
    The monster so appearing
Is sure to really stick
    To memory enduring.

So, if you get a chance to
    Achieve a lucky sighting
Be sure the Loch Ness Monster
    Believes in **YOU!** - (Exciting!)"

J. S. BACH

SO, IF YOU SEE THE MON - STER, LET US KNOW AT ONCE,

FOR A SING - LE SIGHT - ING MAY BE JUST E-NOUGH

TO CON-VINCE YOUR FRIENDS YOU'RE NOT JUST TALKING BLUFF!

(etc.)

GOD'S PORTRAIT

No artist ever painted GOD!
   His brush was never long enough,
Nor found the place of his abode, . . .
   He never could see far enough.

"Depends on what you mean by God"
   Perceived by mortals here below,
So would insist Professor Joad, -   *
   So painted Michaelangelo

Who took aside some model human
   Of visage bearded and benign,
All dressed in flowing robes, assuming
   That clothes must cover forms divine,

Yet recognised his painted homage
    Was but his pallet's pale portrayal,
Creating "God" in mankind's image,
    While seeing it simply as a symbol

Full knowing divinely God resides
    Outwith the bounds of outer-space,
Spares time for us, - and yet abides
    Beyond time's realms, - in timelessness,

And made from stuff that matter isn't, . . .
    What matters most being largely due
To God's true kingdom-come being present
    Within that spirit known as YOU!

Ah! Look no farther, friends, because
    Our servant Science claims and states:
"Each thing created has its cause."
    The First and un-caused Cause CREATES!

*   PROFESSOR JOAD, A FAMED PHILOSOPHER,
    ON B.B.C. "BRAINS-TRUST" OFT BROADCAST
    WAY BACK IN THE FORTIES; NO WORD WOULD HE GLOSS OVER,
    BUT MADE SURE ITS MEANING WOULD HOLD FAST.

VOTING for the POPE

Purely personal impressions of a papal election
as reported in the papers, - April 2005 A.D.

That Conclave of Cardinals recently met
    High up in some Vatican attic
To ponder the problem of who was best bet
    To vote-for in mode democratic.

The previous Pope, having popped off to face
    His Maker in heaven above,
Was heartily hailed a hard man to replace
    Once given that final hard shove.

Suggestions those prelates red-hatted debated
    For quite a considerable time,
Such questions about which they chatted related
    To who'd pose as Pope, next-in-line,

What prestige high-held by qualification?
    Which fellow most fully equipped
To hold Peter's keys, - and come from which nation?
    Upon Peter's chair fit to sit.

Until a large Cardinal pointed a fat finger
    Without undue ritual or ceremony
At one in his bath who was hardly a bad singer
    And came not from Poland but Germany.

Who'd throw in his hat as would any old hat-flinger
    In exchange for a little white skull-cap.
"We could just do worse than choose Joseph Ratzinger
    In theology far from a dull chap."

"What chance has the Church to hold on to hope?"
    Said some sounding strangely aggressive,
"With Ratzinger prancing around as the Pope
    There's no chance for changes progressive?"

Meanwhile a white wisp of the holiest smoke
    Accorded to HIM all authority
Of having been voted the next chosen Pope
    Albeit with slim small majority.

At last after lunch, plus additional cheese,
    Well-stocked behind each umbilica
They chucked him that bunch of traditional keys
    To unlock Saint Peter's Basilica.

************   Meanwhile   ***********

Two cardinals crept to the crypt undetected,
    Avoiding this noise and excitement,
From pomp and from pageantry thus they'd defected
    To privately voice their indictment

Of one they regarded as caretaker-lodger,
    Who'd reign till the crow of a cock;
"Let's waken our hearts to the fact that this codger
    Will do naught but put back the clock!"

"Although Joseph Ratzinger's terribly clever,"
	Went the drift of their chat in the basement,
"We can't see him lasting for ever and ever,
	We should think in advance of replacement."

"Behold all this pompous ridiculous ritual,
	With uniforms all ostentatious!
Just clothed in a loin-cloth hung that Individual
	Condemned to a death so ungracious."

"In plain clothes he peacefully preached those beatitudes;
	What would he have thought of that scene,
Presented by proudly pretentious attitudes
	A welter of wealth quite obscene?"

Now one of the twain held views puritanical
	By many more minus-degrees,
Surveyed all such scenes as somewhat satanical,
	Preferring by far the "Wee Frees". (Strict Scots sect)

"We freeze!" said those Presbies, "yet all of us hope
	To select his successor quite easily,
For once we thaw-out, p'rhaps a protestant Pope
	May emerge - should we choose Ian Paisley?"

"But some may prefer a more moderate man
	To fill that most sacred position
Or a lady perhaps to accord with God's plan
	For women to upset tradition?"

INCREDIBLE BELIEFS

CREDO IN MEUM SOLUM   [I ONLY BELIEVE IN MYSELF]

"Beliefs, oh beliefs! bring nothing but griefs!"
    ["Sir, aren't your words contradiction?
Safeguard what you hold, if that's your belief,
    Until you find sound-based conviction!"]

"Just look at those hooligans, how they behave!
    Self-righteous in vicious derision
Of those with their own pet religion to save,
    'Gainst others creating division.

Division, division, in past times has caused
    One side to draw swords 'gainst the other,
Responsible only for starting such wars
    As on they go, raging for ever.

Religion, religion, out of date I insist!
    It's nothing whatever to do-with-me!
As for God as you call him, he doesn't exist,
    If you think that he does, what's your proof-to-me?

Old-fashioned, old-fashioned, is God by belief,
    Imagined and quite out of date,
Out of date, out of date, good God and good grief!
    And dead as the Dodo, my mate.

What's prayer? What's prayer? Of time what a waste
    Addressing a being that doesn't exist!
Some kneel facing Mecca, you Christians face East,
    Achieving just what? Why must you persist?"

CREDO IN UNUM DEUM   [I BELIEVE IN ONE GOD]

The man who wrote Psalms, wrote Psalms for the thoughtful,
     Stated firmly with feeling impassioned: (Psalm 13)
"In his heart, said the fool, there's **no** God."   But *what* fool
     Is more than that old-fool old-fashioned?

Three thousand years on since that Psalmist prophetic
     Admonished the heathen and heedless,
Men perpetrate still their procedures pathetic
     That goodness (or God) may succeed less.

You say that religion brings war to the world,
     Christianity lies at the back of it!
What false allegation accusing the Lord!
     The commoner cause is the lack of it!

Men love their divisions, find any excuse
     To break up in fragments, form wee sects,
For even in football will warfare break loose,
     Religion misused as a pretext!

Against men with red hair, pink eyes, or dark faces
     Men differing in colour discriminate!
Distinctions unreasoned the bigot's disgrace is
     Under any pretext he'll incriminate.

I don't mean to say, - I don't and I didn't!
     That atheists all are just evil?
By no means! for many are good, wise, and prudent,
     Rejecting the works of the Devil!

But friend, ah my friend! Such a fine self-made man!
     Anti-God, anti-Faith, p'raps God-hater,
Like all self-made men, you've mapped-out your plan,
     To worship your self-made creator!

SOLACE IN CIRCUMSTANCES OF SUFFERING

The Lord of all Love never preached any bitterness,
    Behold how he preached his beatitudes!
Being never invited to come and bear witness
    When mankind was un-kind in attitudes . . .

Went out of his way to commend the Samaritan
    Despised by the proud passer-by,
Who just crossed the road, as the first-aider carried on,
    Content that the injured might die.

He never was there, and was never invited
    To come and preside on occasions
When mankind decided to stand dis-united,
    Despising the next man's persuasions.

He never was there when martyrs were martyred,
    As both sides harsh tortures inflicted
On those whose faith differed, when what really mattered
    Was how their own conscience dictated.

Now where was your God when disaster was making
    Its mark on this world that we run?
"My God! - why, my God, have *I* been forsaken?"
    That question was asked by his Son!

Ah! Naught but a mystery suffering be
    If even God's Son had endured it,
Inevitably sharing some suffering, we
    Know no one who ever had cured it!

Yet, prior to dying, he'd set up a group
    Declaring the cloud's golden lining
Of glorious eternally radiant hope
    Beyond a mere human defining.

CHASTISING THE CHURCH

That group that he never just left in the lurch
    Of ordinary followers consisted
And got themselves organised into a CHURCH
    Which un-truths had since then resisted.

And yet, though many such members proved useless, -
    One even turned treacherous traitor, -
This message of hope, to this day far from news-less
    Relays through its media-creator.

Some perished while preaching but PEACE with discretion,
    Preferring the faith they'd rely on
To meekly accepting some Emperor's oppression,
    Then be munched in the mouth of a lion!

Some still see the Church a little suspiciously,
    So any old stick they find good enough
To beat the old Church with, and beat it as viciously
    As its founder was flogged by thongs rough.

In history's course, some tried to reform
    From without, some internal defects,
But good old Saint Benedict, man of great charm,
    From *within* cleansed its principled precepts.

For Satan will infiltrate all walks of life,
    Paradoxes producing, while seeking
To upset life's balance by untoward strife
    Past man's comprehension, past speaking.

Dear Satan, dear Satan, you've always done well
    At making much mayhem and mischief
You operate still, from your workshop in Hell,
    Of evil-doers always the Big-Chief!

Some QUESTIONS on the BEST ONES
[WITH ONE SELECTED AS AN APT EXAMPLE]

Such scandalous bad news we all hear broadcast widely,
　　But rarely does the media a slot concede
For news that's good, for deeds done well and wisely!
　　Some questions hence of answers stand in need:

Which ancient institution possesses no armed forces
　　Yet forms the voluntary army of free nations? -
While armed régimes can yet be crushed by armed resources,
　　Who ever has destroyed the Army of Salvation?

Who was that four-times Doctor who went off to cure
　　The sick in darkest Africa? - You've guessed it right, sir!
Philosophy, Theology, of Music, and of Medicine sure,
　　Of course it was that four-fold Doctor, Albert Schweitzer.

Who was it knew no class-distinctions, cured the leper,
　　And made the Lord of Love and Science his example?
Biology, Theology, conflicted never
　　To him whose mind and Mission proved so widely ample,

As humbly he'd apply his intellect illustrious,
　　He kept a colony of pets, an hundred ants
In order to observe their antics so industrious
　　Kept under glass, - invading not his under-pants!

Though animals of Africa he loved, revered each life,
　　His "reverence for life" * extending to each creature,
His versatility increased his vision wide　　* [Well-known maxim]
　　To travel far and widely as a Christian preacher,

He daily prayed to God who never could detect
    One single hint of insincere hypocrisy
As Albert raised on high his mighty intellect
    Then put his prayer to practical utility.

Authority on Bach was he, the fact is known,
    His genius musical he'd not let flag nor fail
A rather off-tune keyboard he would practice on
    Then raise more cash for Africa to great avail.

He came to London where, at Barking-by-the-Tower,
    Of Bach's great organ works, "Cathedrals-built-of-Sound",
He made recordings manually, plying pedals hour by hour,
    At Strasbourg also would his organ-playing resound.

He even came to Glasgow to convert its heathen,
    By invitation, - not without their kind permission,
Thus raising funds to help his work of patient healing
    Once back in Africa to medically mind his mission.

Of Saints like Schweitzer, minds both broad and all-embracing,
    We need the more. His talents quite a fortune made
Devoted not to selfish aims, but selflessly full-facing
    The needs of others sick and much less fortunate.

Such facts of life heroic may be little-known,
    In fact, the 'Lives of Saints' may be but little read.
As Shakespeare said, 'The evil that men do lives on,
    The good interréd with their bones,' - once be they dead.

So, as we down our daily diet, do reflect
    While still all's good, we yet make dietary profit,
But should our food go off, submitting to defect,
    Tell him who simply says all's bad, 'Now just come off it!'

NON-BELIEF and BELIEF
(BEST SUNG TO A WELSH TUNE CALLED ST DENIO)

ONLY SEEING IS BELIEVING

Immortal? Invisible? - Questions unwise!
I only believe what's revealed to mine eyes.
You see that old oak-tree that grows in the square?
When no one's about, it is not really there!

What's more, once we snuff it, stone dead we remain,
The same fate awaits all, we'll rise not again.
Whatever our good deeds or crimes we commit,
We'll all end up buried beneath mounds of grit.

Those odd theologians, such nonsense they talk,
Such utter codswollop! Disputes they provoke
Promoting their gospels to spread their strange creeds
With rituals habitual for which we've no need.

BELIEVING: SEEING the UNSEEN

Immortal Invisible, God only wise!
To all unbelievers well-hid from their eyes;
Their lofty opinions they hold high above
The prizes he promised, - rewards sent by Love.

All life is God-given to both great and small,
Existence He's made of, to share with us all.
We blossom and flourish like leaves on the tree
Then wither and perish, - till new life we see!

Unresting, unhasting, and silent as light,
One day he will rescue mankind from its plight.
He promised, beyond this short life that we have,
Repose and reward, as our souls ever live!

FORETHOUGHTS ON THE AFTER-LIFE

Some think there's an after-life; others feel sure of it
To make up for this one, and what we endure of it,
But should one discover on making a tour of it
That I have already arrived, you must face
The fact that you've probably earned the disgrace
Of ending up dwelling in quite the wrong place!

DEATH'S SHARP SCYTHE

When Death's sharp scythe cuts off my head
    Not sharp enough to duck it,
The only thing to be upset
    Will be the proverbial bucket
As by my feet it will be met
    Their last act being to kick it.

Dear friends rejoice! At last I'm free
    From woes and pains of body
Which better served myself than thee
    For which I'm truly sorry.
Dear human race, - my soul with glee
    Says "Good-bye everybody!"

FOREWORD –- at the back!
WHY RHYME? WHY VERSIFY AT ALL?

NOW, CHILDREN, WHAT DO YOU MAKE OF THIS?

Read it carefully:

Coruscate, coruscate, diminutive stellar orb!
How inexplicable to me is the problem of your existence!

And this:

It's a factual matter, my colleagues, a factual matter,
Its veracity is universally acknowledged,
It is invariably a sagacious course of action
To avoid the perpetration of terminological inexactitudes
In order to achieve the result that its authenticity
May be universally acknowledged.

And this too:

Oh, indicate the itinerary to my residence;
I'm fatigued and desire to recline reposefully
In a horizontal position.
I consumed a quantitively diminutive libation
Of an alcoholic beverage sixty minutes ago,
And its effects have penetrated
To the utmost extremities of my cranial cavities!
Irrespective of where I perambulate,
Over territorial areas, over oceanic expanses,
Or over aquatudinous effervescence,
You'll invariably be a witness to my vocally intoning
Of this diminutive melodic incantation:-
Oh! Indicate the itinerary to my residence!

Now, move on to the next page:-

BACK-WORDS - to the fore!

NOW, ADULTS, WOULD THIS NOT MAKE IT A LITTLE EASIER?

Read this carefully; it's not too difficult:-

Twinkle, twinkle, little star;
How I wonder what you are!

[And so on. You know the rest.]

Then try to read this:

It's true, lads, it's true!
Everybody knows it's true.
It's always wise to tell no lies,
So everybody knows it's true.

And finally this:

Oh! Show me the way to go home
I'm tired and I want to go to bed.
I had a little drink about an hour ago,
And it's gone right to my head!
No matter where I roam,
Over land, over sea, over foam,
You'll always hear me sing this little song:
Oh! Show me the way to go home.

NOW, CHILDREN - and even adults - tell us honestly:

Which versions, - on this page - or the one before - make it:
(a) Easier reading? (b) A nicer sound? (c) Possible to go to a
nice tune? (d) Easier to remember? Have you now answered
for yourself the questions just below the FOREWORD at the
back? Have you?

"DEAR MOTHER!
HOW IS IT I HAVE COME TO BE?"

"PLEASE WAIT DEAR BOY, BE PATIENT PLEASE,
MY LITTLE KNOWLEDGE I'LL RELEASE
BY MEANS OF THIS BRIEF NOTE TO THEE."

I bet it seems seldom a young soul expects
A letter containing a lecture on sex,
But this one's devoted to treating as clean
The subject of sex, - as it ever has been
Respectable, - never a topic to scorn,
Without which no being has ever been born.

Yet several souls suffer unseemly defects
By thinking there's something unclean about sex,
Which can't be the case, - for participation
Forms part of that plan, Divine by creation,
To keep this world peopled, though Father's small input
Is feebler by far than your Mother's great output.

For nine caring months, had you grown in her womb
Till time had arrived to accord you more room.
With heart ready beating, your blood red and warm,
Pair of lungs begin breathing, as boy or girl born!
Already your face cries out to be led
To that place of nutrition where straightway you're fed.

Those beautiful breasts of your mother must nourish
You till you can fend for yourself, - and thus flourish!
With features unique, you are sure to inherit,
More miraculous yet, your singular spirit!
Your body it serves as quite indivisible
Till finally released to those realms yet invisible.

Still young, you'd been sent off to school with a cap on
Where one enquires, "How did that miracle happen?"
Look around. Girls abound! Yet different they seem.
In the playground boys shout, while young girlies scream.
Then, once you'd arrived in more advanced classes,
You're certain to ask about lovely young lassies.

So beauteous appearing, they like young lads handsome,
When teenage-time's nearing, girls manage to land some
Like fish in their nets, making personal catchments,
While wishing to get hold of young boys' attachments,
Full-knowing males protrude where females recede,
Life's loving fulfillment seems something they need.

They seem to come closer, those years adolescent,
When physical feelings fair-fizz effervescent
With amorous ambitions, as boys begin dating
Young girls in their teens, - well-warned against mating!
"Till wedding night wait until cutting the cake.
Content yourselves meanwhile with love you may make."

Perhaps playing tennis, or cycling together,
Or go to the Palais to dance and to blether,
Plunge into the pool, improving your swimming,
Each elegant girl knowing it's good for her slimming.
Play games out-of-doors, your choice is whatever
Will help you to get to know each other better.

Such means, so it seems, for all sorts of sporting
Are yours in your teens, for amorous courting,
Till later you're driven by car or by carriage
To finally face the contract of Marriage
When blessed are you both from high heaven above.
By that loveliest luxury in life - namely LOVE!

Printed in the United States
By Bookmasters